Led to Believe by Billy Graham

Led to Believe by Billy Graham

Inspiring Words *from* Billy Graham *and* Others *on* Living *by* Faith

With a Special Reflection from ANNE GRAHAM LOTZ

GuidepostsBooks®
New York, New York

GuidepostsBooks™

Led to Believe by Billy Graham

ISBN-13: 978-0-8249-4726-2

Published by GuidepostsBooks
16 East 34ᵗʰ Street, New York, New York 10016
www.guidepostsbooks.com

Distributed by Ideals Publications, a Guideposts company
535 Metroplex Drive, Suite 250, Nashville, Tennessee 37211

GuidepostsBooks and *Ideals* are registered trademarks of Guideposts, Carmel, New York.

ACKNOWLEDGMENTS

Every attempt has been made to credit the sources of copyrighted material used in this book. If any such acknowledgment has been inadvertently omitted or miscredited, receipt of such information would be appreciated.

"Your Hour of Decision," "Never Quit on a Boy," "Go Ahead and Try!" "The Billy Graham Team," "My Last Chance," "When the Crowd Jeered," "Inside Our Home," "Stormy Hearts," "They Gave Me the Melody," "Baseball Daze, Radio Days," "Billy Graham's Dilemma," "The Truth about Pressure," "A Visit with Billy Graham," "Whatever Happened to Harold?" "The Day My Faith Meant Most to Me," "New Words for the Old, Old Story," "A Brave Tear" and "Out There Somewhere," originally appeared in *Guideposts* magazine; reprinted with permission. "Faith Strengthener" by Billy Graham courtesy of Good News Publishers. "My Father's Message" by Anne Graham Lotz used by permission of the author.

Library of Congress Cataloging-in-Publication Data

Led to believe by Billy Graham / inspiring words from Billy Graham and others on living by faith ; with a special reflection from Anne Graham Lotz.
    p. cm.
  ISBN 978-0-8249-4726-2
1. Graham, Billy, 1918- 2. Evangelistic work. 3. Christian life. 4. Faith. I. Graham, Billy, 1918- II. Guideposts Associates.
  BV3785.G69L43 2007
  248.2'4--dc22

2007007399

Jacket and interior design by Marisa Jackson.
Cover photograph © Everett Collection

Printed and bound in the United States of America

10 9 8 7 6 5 4 3 2 1

Contents

Introduction

What happens after your heart has been changed forever—after Billy Graham has led your heart to believe that God loves you and wants you to walk with Him every day?

Billy Graham's passionate ministry, spanning over six decades, has helped millions of people accept a God-centered way of life. His call appealed to each of those men and women in a unique way—one heart at a time. *Led to Believe by Billy Graham* is a touching collection of this beloved preacher's own words and beliefs, interwoven with stories from real people whose lives were changed by his message.

In the first revealing piece, Billy Graham recalls how his own life changed when he decided to be a "living, breathing worker for God." The commitment of this one man has made a spiritual difference for so many, and it sets the tone for the personal stories in this section, which show, as Rev. Graham says, "what God can do with a person."

In another reflection, Billy Graham describes himself as a preacher whose job is to "faithfully proclaim, to pray, to sow the seed" and then leave the Holy Spirit to work on a person's heart. He often didn't know what generated and bloomed as a result of his work. As you read his words at the beginning of each section in this book, you will have an opportunity to connect his efforts to call the world back to God with real stories of people who listened to that call and were changed. A young journalist pours out her fears in prayer and reveals the depth of her faith to the one she loves, even as she expects his scorn. An ex-convict finds the courage to turn his back on crime and rebuild his life. A suffering woman asks God one last time for her disease to be healed, and somehow knows He will answer her prayer.

From the amazingly miraculous to quiet manifestations, the experiences of both well-known and little-known people are here—their changed hearts, renewed purpose and the challenging, but ultimately rewarding, choices they made. Each reveals what happened when

Billy Graham led them to listen for God's voice, and they tried to live by it. One big league pitcher learns to look to God for peace and strength, instead of being led by his own ego. A radio news announcer who never knew his mother is finally reunited with her, after an event makes them both trust in God's perfect timing. And in an unforgettable example of the minister being ministered to, a badly wounded soldier's faith and gratitude give Billy Graham an inspirational moment he will always cherish. As a final tribute, Billy Graham's daughter Anne Graham Lotz recalls a moment in her teenage life when her father's love and concern taught her a moving lesson about her heavenly Father.

It is our hope that these lives will inspire you just as these men and women were inspired by Billy Graham's call to walk on God's path. We hope the words and thoughts of Rev. Graham and those who heard his message will help you find hope and strength in your own faith walk.

The Editors

PART I

What God Can Do

Your Hour of Decision

Billy Graham

People come up to me and say: "Why should I make a decision about God? I'm happy doing what I'm doing. You call it sin—I call it fun. Live and let live."

If they don't say it in these words, the thought's there unspoken, in their faces.

There's pleasure in sin—but only for a season. Deep down there is a gnawing, dull dissatisfaction.

I sat down with a sixty-nine-year-old business executive in a large Eastern city recently who told me, "I have fifty million dollars and everything I could ever want— and I am the most miserable man in this city."

One of the biggest names in Hollywood, a tall, strapping, swashbuckling type, revealed the same thing in different words. His life, he admitted, was lonely and empty.

These are two prominent people who have discovered that wealth and fame aren't enough in life. Millions more feel the same way. Telling lies and dodging the facts cannot shield them from the real truth—that because their consciences are black with acts against God, they can find no inner peace. To cleanse out this dirt, they need the injection of a driving spiritual force in their lives.

Jim Vaus came out of World War II a master of electronics. Within a few years he was in the employ of big gamblers on the West Coast, drawing down huge fees for his craftsmanship at wiretapping and communications.

One night Jim dropped in on one of our meetings in Los Angeles to kill time before he was to take off by plane for a very important deal in St. Louis. Outwardly indifferent, he stood at the rear of the hall. When the call came for those in the audience to come forward and make a decision for Christ, something clicked inside of Jim Vaus. His face twisted with emotion, he started walking to the front of the hall. Jim then made a decision to break clean with his old life and contacts. Today, he is one of the Lord's hardest workers.

Jim Vaus found out later that the plane he didn't

catch during that night of decision was met in St. Louis by gunmen who had instructions to kill him.

This is a spectacular example of what God can do with a person. Hundreds of men and women are reborn, less dramatically, at every meeting.

"But, Billy," some people say, "what do you mean by being born again?"

To be born again means that the Divine Life has entered the human soul. God's objective then is to have that person start life anew, living in the image of His Son, Jesus Christ. The two conditions of this rebirth are repentance toward God and faith toward Christ.

At our meetings that emphasize the family and home, whole families have come forward to make their decision together.

Once a husband and wife, who had parted, came to the meeting separately. He started forward at the end. So did she. Startled, they met face to face, then joined hands with tears in their eyes.

We hold these meetings over periods of four to eight weeks in cities and towns, usually where we have received a joint invitation from the churches in the community. The effectiveness of our meetings, we have found, depends on working with local churches and ministers and giving them the responsibility of following up our efforts with a program of their own.

The results so far have been heartening—for which we give God the glory. Our continuing prayer in these days is that we can remain in a position of usefulness to God and play a part in calling the world back to Him before it is too late.

If you are a disbeliever, a skeptic or just indifferent, I know what you're going through. I've gone through it all myself. If you feel that you are just naturally weak, let me assure you that many persons who once were weak, today are the strongest workers for God. The Scripture says that strength comes from weakness.

When I wandered into my first revival meeting back in 1934 in Charlotte, North Carolina, I was a gangling kid of sixteen with a consuming ambition to be a major league ball player. The last thing I wanted to be was a preacher. From our worldly crowd, two of us, Grady Wilson and I, went to the meeting to see what the shouting was about.

The first night I hid behind a stout lady's big hat. I recall vividly the smell of pine shavings in my nostrils . . .

also the strange stirrings that churned up inside me to know more about Christ. Although my family had reared me in a fine religious background, I had shrugged off much of it during this particular period of teenage restlessness.

The second night I sat up closer and battled with the questions everyone asks. Was it sissified to embrace Christ? Could you be religious and still have fun? Who would be looking if I were to go forward at the end of the meeting? Why couldn't I make a decision without walking all the way to the front?

All these questions are rooted in man's pride and egotism. God didn't come through to me as a real Presence until I publicly made the decision to be a living, breathing worker for God. *Not an evangelist though,* I said to myself.

Months later, after some of the most exhaustive prayer sessions I have ever had, I decided to make religion my career.

To earn enough money to pay my way through Bible school, I spent one summer selling brushes. This experience taught me that regardless of whether I offered brushes or faith in God, without personal convictions and enthusiasm I was wasting my time.

Being jilted at eighteen made a terrific impact on me. The fact that the girl in question said she didn't think I would amount to anything helped light a fire under me. After a long session of self-analysis, I decided I did want to amount to something—not for myself but for God.

While attending the Florida Bible Institute, I began to practice preaching in a nearby wood. Almost daily I would slip into the swampland, lay my notes on a stump and offer my sermon to the birds, alligators, frogs and all who would listen.

Then came the question that nags many who start out doing God's work. "How do I know God wants me to do this?"

The only way I knew I could get an answer was through prayer. "God," I said, "if You want me to preach, help me locate a pulpit."

That same day a man came up to me, said he had heard me preaching and asked if I would give a sermon at a gospel meeting that night down the road. This—my first real answer to prayer—started my career for the Lord.

Today when a cynic asks me "How does giving your life to God pay off?" or "If I change, what will God do for me?" I can answer by telling him what He has done for me.

He forgave my sins; He gave me peace of mind; He took away my fear of death. He stirred up creative powers within me that I never realized existed. But more important than what I received from God are the efforts I have since been able to make for Him.

Billy and Daddy

Daniel Schantz

When my father tuned the Motorola car radio to *The Hour of Decision*, everyone grew quiet. I was eleven that year, 1953, and the Graham crusades were in full stride. On Sunday nights after church, my preacher father Edward would herd us into our '49 Chevy Bel Air and take us for a slow drive through the magical darkness of the northern Indiana countryside, stopping only at the dairy for an ice cream cone. I would hang my head out the window so I could feel the cool evening air and smell the newly mowed hay. I was captivated by the crescendo of crickets and frogs that rose from the ditches, but when I heard Billy Graham, in his North Carolina accent, welcome his listeners to "The Owl-wah of Duhsizzun," I pulled my head inside.

Never mind that I had already heard two sermons from my father. When Billy spoke, everyone listened.

"Billy Graham is an orator," my Dad said, but I wasn't sure what that was. He clarified. "His voice is like a trumpet. He reminds me of the old time prophets, like Amos and Isaiah. When he speaks, people get goosebumps." I grinned and checked my arms for goosebumps. "Billy is not afraid to use the word *sin*, Dad added. "And I like the way he always calls for decisions. There's no sense preaching a powerful sermon if you don't close the sale."

It was not irreverent to refer to Billy Graham as "Billy." Seems like everyone in America did, and it was a tribute, not a slight.

"Billy has a lot of help," Dad pointed out, a touch of envy in his voice. "He has a large staff and talented performers, like George Beverly Shea.

"And a very nice wife," my mother injected, and Dad winked at me.

When "Bev" Shea sang, "How Great Thou Art," my father hummed along with him, and when the song was over, Dad let out a long sigh, as if he himself were George Beverly, singing on stage.

I knew my father didn't have much help. He never had a secretary. He ran the office all by himself, cranked out a weekly church paper and made all the sick calls

alone. And I knew that there were thousands of preachers like my dad, who prepared the way for Billy Graham
crusades, by conducting surveys and passing out flyers.
They enlisted ushers and counselors, and followed up
the meetings with personal contacts and baptisms. I had
heard my father talk about them.

"I'll say this for Billy," my mother spoke up. "There
has never been a scandal about him. He practices what
he preaches." She had seen too many preachers brought
down by the love of money or women.

There was never any scandal about my handsome
father either, even though Mom was no Madison Avenue
model, and we needed money desperately.

Dad turned down the radio to make a point. "Billy
sticks to the basics, that's his strength. Too many big time
preachers are into psychology. Health-and-wealth gospel.
Billy says our problem is sin, and we need to repent." I
nodded. Even at eleven years old, I knew that much.

My father didn't agree with everything Billy said,
but he sensed that there was a need for a preacher like
him who could serve notice to a jaded world that it had
made a wrong turn. Someone with access to radio and
television.

Near the end of the *Hour of Decision*, Dad listened with a special intensity when the narrator described the many in the audience who were coming forward to make a decision for Christ. When the audience sang, "Just as I am, without one plea . . ." I could see tears in my father's eyes, and I was reminded that my father's whole life was geared toward such moments.

At the end of the program, Billy Graham would urge listeners to write to him. "Write to me, Billy Graham, Minneapolis, Minnesota. That's all the address you need." My father said that it was even easier than that. "All you have to do," he explained, "is to write the name 'Billy Graham' on an envelope and drop it in the mailbox, and he will get it. Billy knows everybody in the world, even presidents and kings. And everybody knows him."

I was impressed, but I didn't personally know Billy, and I did know my father very well. I knew that he had everything but fame. Never competitive, Dad was content to be just "Ed," minister to a tiny congregation in the little town of Harlan, Indiana, just outside of Fort Wayne.

When, at last, Dad clicked off the radio, we rode home in sweet silence. Snuggled in the back seat with my brothers, and savoring a ten-cent ice cream cone, I was at peace with the world. The words of Billy Graham played over and over in my little mind. "What the world needs most is Jesus Christ," and I was glad that I had found Christ when my own father baptized me into Christ at the age of eight.

I looked at my handsome father with pride. His rugged hands gripped the wheel, and his wise eyes guided us through a maze of country roads, toward home. At such times, I had no doubt who was the greatest preacher in the world, and I know that even Billy Graham would agree with me on that.

Billy, meet Dad.

Never Quit on a Boy

Jim Vaus

One of the biggest stories of our time—or any time—is the perplexing problem of rebellious boys and girls who get in trouble and break the hearts of their parents and close friends. In the six years that I have worked with teenagers around and about New York City's East Side, I have experienced that heartache many times. Yet I also have learned this:

Never quit on any human being no matter how bad things seem.

Take the boy they called the Cardinal. I first met him in 1959 when he was head of a gang known as The Untouchables.

The Cardinal was tough, proud, clever. A junior in high school at the time, the Cardinal never knew his mother and lived with his grandmother. Behind his arrogant face I could read the usual teenage signs of confusion, frustration and hurt.

I talked to him one day about our Youth Center and the Christian purpose behind it. "As far as I'm concerned," he said, "church is a place for punks, and Jesus Christ is nothing but a good swear word."

And that ended our first conversation! Yet how much of myself did I see in the Cardinal?

Until I was almost thirty years old, I had been at war with the world. From the age of ten I was a cheat, a thief and a fraud. All this changed one remarkable night in 1949 when I found myself on my knees at a Billy Graham meeting, pledging my life to Jesus Christ.

During the following months when I tried to undo some of my wrongs and receive forgiveness for the others, I began to give talks at various churches, clubs and institutions. After telling my story to a group of inmates at the Eastern State Penitentiary in Pennsylvania, a boy, serving a life sentence for killing a policeman, came up to me afterward. "You should have talked to us about Jesus Christ before we got here," he said wistfully.

It was a jolt that I needed. A few months later I was involved in long discussions with Police Captain

Conrad Jensen of the 23rd Precinct in New York City. This precinct had one of the highest rates of juvenile crime in the city—a cesspool of violence, corruption, drug addiction, prostitution, thievery and poverty.

I told the captain of my plan to start a youth center that would combine recreation, crafts and religion. "I'm not here as some do-gooder," I said. "My purpose is to win a hearing for Christ and His Gospel. I am convinced that when His love is felt, He will be heard."

Captain Jensen was encouraging. He said, "I've been praying for months, if not years, that God would send someone like you here."

The first youth development center was opened in a store. No one came around. So I put on a science show featuring electronic equipment in a local public school; after this, nine kids came to the store. When they told me who the gang leaders were in the area, I went after them. If the life of one leader could be redirected, he in turn could help redirect the lives of all those who followed him.

Progress was slow, painfully slow. The Cardinal was typical of the scorn most teenagers felt toward a project that smacked of religion.

But the Cardinal had a curious nature. He wanted to

know more about the electronic equipment set up in the center. He was curious about the Sunday program we had of rounding up the boys at 8:00 AM for a bus trip downtown for Sunday school services. He wanted to know about the membership card, which each boy needed to participate in our program.

One day he asked for a card. "You'll have to wait two months," I told him. This trial period gave me a chance to learn about the boy, his haunts and habits. The Cardinal was incensed that he would have to wait and stormed off. But he came back again. At the end of two months he received his membership.

On the very next Sunday he joined us on the morning bus ride to Sunday school services. A year later he was elected president of the Sunday school class. "I want to give my heart to Jesus Christ," he told all of us. There was no doubt about the change that had taken place in this boy. He had won a victory over the evil in himself. He had become a leader. And it is at this point, I've discovered, that new Christians can be most vulnerable.

The Cardinal was on his way home several days later when he ran into some of his old friends. They were waiting for him.

"Here's the boy who's gone to Jesus," taunted one.

"How does it feel to be so holy?"

"Hey, punk, gowan back to church," said another.

"We're going to heist a store."

The sneers, the contempt got under the Cardinal's skin. The blood rushed to his head. He snarled back at them. They laughed. "Come with us—or get out of our sight," they finally told him.

The seventeen-year-old Cardinal wasn't the first to buckle under the pressure. He joined them.

I was in court several days later when the four boys— Scoop, Zip, Soapy and the Cardinal—stood before the judge awaiting sentence. They had broken through the ceiling of a store, unknowingly tripped an alarm, then walked out with some $2,400 worth of merchandise— right into the arms of two policemen with drawn guns.

Zip and Soapy, who admitted hatching the plot, were given jail sentences. The Cardinal and Scoop received three years of probation and were paroled in my custody. And so you begin all over. Discouragement is a luxury you cannot afford.

The three of us sat in my office, and I told them the story of my own life of petty crime. "I never had the ability or strength to change myself," I said. "No man can—alone. But what I couldn't do, Jesus Christ did. If you're ever going to amount to anything, you must get this thought planted in your thick heads: I can do all things through Christ which strengtheneth me.

"When the judge says, 'You're guilty,' that's it. You pay the penalty, but you may end up in a life of crime and a dead-end street. When the Lord tells us we're guilty, we pay the penalty also. But there is no dead-end street. For He forgives us and gives us a chance to make amends for what we have done wrong. It's not easy. You'll get some sneers, as the Cardinal discovered. But you have Christ's promise that He will be with you, that He won't forsake you. But it won't work unless you make Him your leader."

On the following Sunday the Cardinal rejoined his Sunday school class. He was quiet and reflective. At the end of the service he asked to say a prayer. I'll never forget it:

"Please God, forgive me for letting You down. I don't know why I was so stupid. I know I need You in my life. And forgive Scoop here who doesn't know how to pray yet. Please look out for Zip and Soapy too. Help us to learn how to live to please You."

It wasn't hard to get Scoop a job. He had no previous record. But it took two years before the Cardinal found employment. It came one day when a friend simply asked if I knew a boy who needed a job. My friend is a banker. So I had to tell him all about the Cardinal, but I also told him that I had great faith in the boy.

All my friend said was, "Let's try."

The Cardinal has been working in the bank for two years now, handling valuable documents, securities and cash. In a department of thirteen people he is now second in line for promotion. He has paid for all the damage done to the store at the rate of five dollars a week, and is completing high school by attending five nights a week. Recently his department boss, who knows all about him, wrote, "We'll take all you can send us of this kind of boy."

And when I read that I got down on my knees and thanked God for His grace. The Cardinal is living proof that God still changes lives.

Not everything comes out roses here in the 23rd. There are as many failures as there are winners, maybe more failures. During the first year of Youth Development there were three spectacular deaths by gang activity. After the second year there were none, not even a serious injury. The crime rate among juveniles in the heart of the area we serve dropped twenty percent from 1958 through 1962.

Recently, a young fellow we had tried to help was picked up by the police for stealing a car. Discouraged, I told myself there was no hope for him. Then I remembered the Cardinal and the lesson he taught me: never quit on a boy.

Go Ahead and Try!

Lela Gilbert

I sat in the Los Angeles Coliseum that evening in September 1963, absently looking around at the tens of thousands of people who had come to hear Billy Graham. I had grown up in the Baptist church, so I didn't expect to learn anything new. After all, I'd listened to the Gospel my whole life, and it had not transformed my miserable existence. I was sixteen, and I suffered constantly from the itching, peeling and disfigurement of a skin disease that had robbed me of a happy childhood and adolescence.

I don't remember the message that night. Yet at the end of the service I found myself moving toward the front of the crowd to rededicate myself, even though I was in anything but a reverent mood.

"Fine," I told the Lord, rather sardonically. "Go ahead

and take control of my life. If You think You can make things better, go right ahead." What a cold and insolent approach that was. But oh, how I needed His touch, inside and out.

I couldn't remember a time when I hadn't been in pain.

"Stop scratching!" My mother must have ordered me to leave my tortured skin alone a dozen times a day. And every time she said those words, I felt guilty. Her face was always unhappy when she saw the red, swollen affliction that covered more than ninety percent of my body.

Some doctors called it eczema. Others identified it as atopic dermatitis. It was caused by allergy. Or it was psychosomatic. Or it was stress related. Countless dermatologists made fascinating observations. But not one found a remedy.

My mother told me the symptoms had appeared when I was six weeks old. Was it the orange juice? Or the formula that replaced mother's milk? Or my father's departure for overseas? Colic accompanied the rash, creating an emotional crisis for my mother, a Navy wife of thirty-five who had never dreamed of having a child so late in life. She was frightened and alone in the new experience of motherhood. Unfortunately, the night-mare was only beginning.

In elementary school I often appeared in class with smelly, sticky, yellow Aureomycin ointment on my arms, neck and legs, and was usually on a strict diet. But I was considered a brain, and therefore survived the critical scrutiny of my classmates.

Then, after my parents consulted with my teacher, it was decided I was doing so well that I should skip the rest of fourth grade. My fifth-grade teacher resented the responsibility of having a student with special needs in her class. It took my new classmates little time to declare me an outcast.

I learned quickly. I was placed in junior high at ten and high school at twelve. They were cruel years. My eczema flared up dramatically. Some mornings my eyes were swollen nearly shut. My nightclothes stuck to the lesions on my arms and legs, and my hair tangled in the scabs that formed around my ears and neck. I constantly applied baby cream, which relieved some of the discomfort but left a layer of greasy residue on my clothes and sheets.

Along with my physical problems, I developed a bit-ter, cynical spirit. I hated my middle-aged, fundamentalist

Christian parents. I resented my mocking schoolmates. Most of all, I despised myself.

So when I made my journey down the aisle at the Billy Graham Crusade, I didn't expect anything to change. In fact, after my rude challenge to God, my skin problem raged on, sometimes aggravated by staph infections. But I noticed an unfamiliar sensation that could almost have been mistaken for euphoria. I was happy all the time. I annoyed people by singing on our college bus. I laughed too loudly, too often. It was immature behavior, but for me it was miraculous.

I began to write poetry. Perhaps it was a gift God gave me to help sort out my muddled emotions. In any case, I fell in love with words, and found voice for my despair.

Although I had several male friends, my romantic life was nonexistent. A boy, who out of kindness had taken me to a football game, handed me a pile of coins one day and pointed toward a pay phone. "You'd better call your doctor," he said. "You look awful."

By twenty I had a number of female friends, and I was respected by the boys who managed to get me to write their term papers for them. But I turned down invitations to spend the night with girlfriends; I didn't want them to know about the scalding showers at midnight, the trail of skin flakes that followed me everywhere, the insane itching that drove me to use plastic combs to scratch myself.

One night nearly four years after my first agreement with God, I was walking alone when a renegade thought entered my mind:

I want to heal your skin!

My religious background had not prepared me to listen to inner voices. Our church taught that God spoke only through the Bible.

"Leave me alone!" I said. "I've learned to live with it. Just leave me alone."

I want to heal your skin. The thought was clearer than before.

"I don't want to think about it! Don't you understand? False hope will make living with this impossible!"

I want to heal your skin.

"Leave me alone!"

And so the dialogue continued. Was it my subconscious? Was I losing my mind? Or was it my Creator?

I stormed into our apartment. "Mother, I think God just told me He wants to heal my skin!"

She looked at me in utter disbelief. "What do you mean He told you?"

"I mean a thought kept coming to me on the way home that said, 'I want to heal your skin.'"

"Well, just don't get your hopes up," she said, shaking her head.

I went to my room, closed the door and got on my knees, feeling like a fool. The chances were slim that God had been talking to me. Why now? Why had He waited so long? Or was my imagination playing cruel tricks on me?

"God, I don't know if You're trying to tell me something or not," I whispered, "but if it's You, great. Go ahead and try . . ."

A week later I revisited our family doctor. He prescribed a medication that had no effect. He referred me to another doctor. Again, nothing. He recommended a new dermatologist. I made an appointment with her, determined that this would be the last time I ever sought healing of my skin.

A few days before my appointment, patches of clear skin began to appear on my arms. "That figures," I grumbled. "She'll never see it at its worst."

And she didn't. Despite the fact that I was taking no medication now, the clear patches grew larger. By the time I arrived at the doctor's office my skin had improved dramatically. Three days later, following the application of a couple of new corticosteroid ointments, my skin was completely clear. It was soft and pink, and there were no scars.

For weeks afterward, I had terrifying dreams of the disease's reappearance. Mornings found me studying the mirror, searching for recurring blemishes. They never came.

But God wasn't finished. I got a job doing clerical work at a large department store in Los Angeles, where I frequently assisted the models backstage at fashion shows.

One of LA's best-known African American models took the time to show me how to walk and turn on a fashion show runway, insisting, "You can do it too!"

Unbelievably, I was soon out on the runway, battling stage fright and insecurity, but striding along to music, dressed in fine suits and fabulous gowns. Gradually I learned to accept myself as a new person, transformed by a caring Father's hand. Sometimes I saw my parents sitting in the audience, amazed at their daughter's metamorphosis.

Today I am far removed from that lonely young girl with the unsightly skin disease. But I will never forget what I learned because of those years: get up and get going, no matter how painful the circumstances, and show compassion to the diseased and the despairing.

And there is one other thing I will never forget: It's alright to get my hopes up, when God is at work.

PART 2

Where God Leads

The Billy Graham Team

Len LeSourd

This *Guideposts* reporter flew to Memphis last June to obtain a firsthand account of the Billy Graham campaign in that city.

"Billy's doing a real job," said the cabbie who drove me to the hotel. "I'm one of the ushers at the auditorium. Pack in about eleven thousand every night."

There are eight members of the Graham team . . . average age thirty-two. I was captured by their tremendous enthusiasm and sense of mission.

Jerry Beavan, the team's executive secretary, took me on a fast tour of campaign headquarters. There was constant excitement. Would Billy do a broadcast from a plane? . . . What about a meeting in the football stadium? . . . The cotton exchange wanted Billy to give them a pep talk. . . .

Religion to the Graham team is not mournful, but a challenge; they feel part of a crusade—an irresistible force. I could just as well have been in the clubhouse of a winning ball team on a pennant drive. The talk was full of zip; their clothes bright. They win people by their enthusiasm and sparkle as well as by their cause, which they know can't be beaten.

Some articles about Billy tell of people running forward wailing and sobbing after meetings shouting, "Hallelujah." The ones I attended had none of this. To be sure, there was emotion as hundreds made decisions. Yet it was dignified. Billy himself discourages outbursts.

Their campaigns feature what may turn out to be a revolutionary follow-up plan on converts. After meetings, those who come forward are led into counseling rooms where hundreds of trained lay workers take over.

The cards filled out are distributed among local churches for future follow-up on the part of laypersons and ministers. The training of laypeople is a very important feature in every campaign. I attended the meeting for men at 6:45 AM. Over two hundred were there, despite the early hour.

These volunteers are told that helping people

make their decision for God is only five percent. "Working on this decision makes up the other ninety-five," the instructor states. Then he outlines a specific plan of action.

Before he goes to a city, Billy asks united support from local ministers—also that a local committee draw up the budget. The Graham team sets no fee; the committee decides everything. Billy does insist that collections at meetings stop when the budget has been raised. After the campaign, a complete financial statement must be published in the local paper.

"The Lord teaches us how to conquer the need for money," says Billy. For example, their radio program (*The Hour of Decision*, Sunday afternoon, ABC network) was started through contributions.

Their teamwork synchronizes perfectly during meetings. Cliff Barrows starts it off with a lively hymn sing. Caught up by his infectious grin, ten thousand people, plus the one-thousand-voice choir, join in enthusiastically.

Soloist George Beverly Shea (RCA Victor recording artist), pianist Tedd Smith and organist Paul Mickelson blend their musical talents. Grady Wilson, associate evangelist, tirelessly speaks and counsels day and night. Willis Haymaker handles advance campaign preparations.

Organization goes into every phase of the campaign. There are babysitters near the main assembly hall, special noonday meetings held daily in the city, and the constant accumulation of statistics (attendance at Graham meetings are now in the millions, converts in the tens of thousands).

I spent most of the day with Billy as he made one appearance after another. Billy speaks to and for all creeds. He attacks no one; his main enemies are sin and communism. Nor does he claim his type of religious work is the most important—only that it is the field where God led him.

Billy feels God is pleased by such facts as these reported from Shreveport, Louisiana, during their campaign there: liquor sales down forty percent, Bible sales up three hundred percent.

My Last Chance . . .

Jim Vaus

I saw them out the nursery window: the black sedan, the four men in dark suits walking toward the house with their hands in their pockets. And behind them was Andy—Andy, who had told me over the phone, "Nobody quits on Andy. Understand what I mean?"

I picked up the baby and handed him to my wife Alice.

"I've got visitors," I said. "You stay back out of sight."

With my mind working desperately, I ran to the front door and threw it open, praying: "Lord, help me make this convincing."

"Andy!" I said. I saw his face tighten. The hand in his pocket moved slightly.

"Well, I guess you heard what happened to me. What do you think of it?"

We stood talking on the front steps for an hour. Andy never took his hand out of his pocket. When, finally, I had told him all there was to tell, he still didn't move. The men with him grew restless; they shifted from one foot to another, waiting.

Then, suddenly, Andy turned his back on me and walked with quick steps to his car. He got in, closed the door, started the motor. I stayed on the front steps. At the last minute, he opened the door again. My heart stopped.

"Jim . . ." Andy said. "Good luck, Jim. I kinda wish I was you."

He drove off.

Andy kinda wished he was me. I wondered . . .

From the earliest days that I can remember, my goal in life was to enter the ministry. This is what my mother prayed that I should do, even before I was born, and though there were times when I thought of following my fondness and natural aptitude for electronics, nothing ever seriously deterred me from my primary purpose. However, as a preministerial student at the Bible Institute of Los Angeles, something happened that completely changed my life.

I had been given the responsible job of handling the funds for the college annual. As part of the campaign, I arranged for a huge rally where students at Biola would talk via radio to missionaries in Africa, China, South America. There'd be a collection but no admission charge.

Everything went well, except for the finances. More than three thousand people from all over Los Angeles came to the rally. I thought they would contribute at least one thousand dollars, but the next morning I was given a check for $92.74.

Stunned and angered, I went back to my room. What I did next was to affect my life for years to come. Was I getting even with the school? Was I denying my family? Was I running away from the ministry? I don't know. I only know that I packed my bags, walked down to the bank, cashed the $92.74 check and then withdrew all the other money that had been entrusted to me for the college annual.

On the plane rushing through the night, I planned the spree I was going to have in Florida. But even as I thought of the sumptuous hotel room, of the girls, of the high living, I knew it would not be this way. When I got off in Miami, the first thing I did was to telephone my father, tell him what I had done, and ask for his advice. His reply was a crisp but not unkind, "Come home."

I expected to be punished. But I did not expect to be punished as severely as I was. I borrowed money and repaid every cent I had stolen. Biola accepted the funds and expelled me. I was told never to set foot on the campus again. An outcast, desperately lonely, I went from bad to worse and finally sank so far that I attempted a stickup—I was caught and sent to prison.

Pearl Harbor brought amnesty to prisoners who would volunteer for the Army. I remember how disgusted I was with the old Jim Vaus, how determined I was to change.

"I'm going to make sergeant," I said to my parents as I left.

They smiled and when my father spoke, there was conviction in his voice. "I'm sure you will, Jim."

As a matter of fact I not only made sergeant, I invented a computer that greatly improved antiaircraft firing, and was promoted to captain.

And then I was court-martialed.

The court-martial read ". . . diverting government property to his own private use . . ." It was true.

I was so ashamed of myself for being in prison again that I went to extreme ends to keep my friends, especially Alice, one very lovely young girl I had met, from discovering the truth.

After the war, I married Alice. For two years I made an effort to keep my personal life clean. I set myself up in business as a consulting electronics engineer. Then, one day I was approached by Mickey Cohen, the man the Los Angeles papers called the "Vice Lord of the West Coast."

"I understand you have been doing some work for the police," said Mickey. "I understand you're a genius at bugging a house. Do you think you could find a bug in my place?"

I tried to explain to Mickey that my specialty was installing wiretap devices, not discovering them. Mickey took out a very large roll of hundred dollar bills and began peeling them off.

"Don't you think you could be persuaded to try?" he said. And from that moment I was working officially for the underworld.

Andy came into the picture. Andy was a bookmaker. He had a great idea; he wanted me to design an electrical device that he could use for beating the races. He wanted me to go into partnership with him. My retainer was more money than I had ever seen before. The profits would be fantastic.

"St. Louis next Monday morning," said Andy. "Eight o'clock at the airport."

Things were going great. That night I told Alice that I'd be away from home for a few days. Alarm came into her eyes.

"How many days, Jim?" She was expecting a baby at any moment.

"I don't know. A few . . ." Alice lowered her eyes and was silent.

The next morning was Sunday, November 6, 1949, the day before I was supposed to take off for St. Louis. Alice was silent at breakfast. I tried to cheer her up by promising her a day at the beach.

"All right," she answered. But with little enthusiasm.

We drove out to the beach in my brand new Cadillac convertible. Alice was subdued. When we got to the beach, she didn't want to get out of the car. We drove on, aimlessly. Up ahead there seemed to be some kind of traffic jam.

"Look," said Alice. "It's Billy Graham." There was enthusiasm in her voice for the first time since I'd announced my trip to St. Louis. I wanted to humor her, so I asked her if she'd like to go hear Graham.

"Yes," she said. "I'd like it very much."

We went inside the Big Tent. I was very uncomfortable. I didn't like the people I saw there.

Graham seemed to be talking directly to me. His text was "What does it profit a man if he gains the whole world and loses his soul?" Could he really be talking to me? Of course not . . . that was just a pulpit trick. I tried to leave, but Alice sat in rapt attention and I didn't dare disturb her. Graham continued to look directly at me. It was too much.

"I'm leaving," I whispered to Alice and started to rise from my seat, but Graham had begun to pray.

"Every head bowed," he said. "Every eye closed. No one moving or leaving . . ."

I couldn't escape; I couldn't even leave when Graham began the call to come forward. Why? Because once again he spoke directly to me. "There's a man here tonight who has heard all this before," he said. I felt my flesh crawl. "There's a man here tonight who knows I am talking to him, who is hardening his heart. With pride he stiffens his neck and he is determined to leave without making a decision. But for that man, this will be his last chance!"

In that instant, God-given conviction gripped my heart. Attempts at reform had failed. I lacked inner power to overcome evil. I believed in a God and the Bible, but I had never accepted Christ or submitted to His authority. I made up my mind, definitely, firmly. There was another call to come forward.

"Alice?" I said. Alice looked at me. There were tension lines around her eyes as if she was trying not to cry. "Let's go, Alice."

Dutifully, Alice got up and worked her way to the aisle ahead of me. At the aisle she turned toward the rear of the tent.

"Alice," I called. "No . . . I meant let's go forward."

Alice looked at me, not understanding. Was I playing a joke on her? Gently I took her by the arm and together we walked forward and there we knelt and we prayed . . . In my prayer I asked Jesus Christ to be my Savior and Master.

Nothing in my life has been the same since that moment. The change was instantaneous, complete, mysterious. The next day I telephoned Andy to say I wouldn't be going to St. Louis. Andy's reply was a blunt: "Nobody quits on Andy. Understand what I mean?"

The next day Alice's labor began. We rushed to the hospital. There'd be big bills to pay, but I knew I couldn't pay them with money I had made dishonestly.

It was shortly after I'd brought Alice and the baby home that Andy drove up in his black limousine and, bolstered only by a prayer, I had gone to face him. How well I remember his parting words: "Jim," he said. "Good luck, Jim, I kinda wish I was you."

One day I was telling my story before a group in Los Angeles. When I had finished, an elderly lady stood up. "Mr. Vaus," she said. "The day after the meeting, you were planning to go to St. Louis?"

"Yes."

"Well, I work in the mayor's office," she went on. "I think you'd be interested to know that on the day you were supposed to fly to St. Louis, we got a teletype from the FBI. Mr. Vaus, that teletype said there was a rival gang waiting for you in St. Louis. You were to be killed on sight."

Blessed Assurance

Roberta Messner

*O*ur living room was empty except for the old upright piano that spring afternoon in May 1964. Mother was in the middle of a wallpapering spree. It was cabbage roses everywhere you looked. As I scooted across the piano bench to play a hymn out of my new book, the familiar melody of "Blessed Assurance" bounced off the walls, mocking me. *You don't have that blessed assurance, Roberta,* it seemed to say. *You've never asked Jesus into your heart like Mr. Graham, that evangelist on TV, says you need to do.*

I should have been thrilled to be playing that song. After all, this was the first week that I'd added my left hand to my piano repertoire. Just a few days ago, my piano teacher had taught me how, and even though the key of D had two sharps, she believed I was up to the task.

I'd chosen "Blessed Assurance" as my hymn for the week because I knew they would be singing it at the Grady Wilson Evangelistic Crusade being held at the Fairfield Stadium in my hometown of Huntington, West Virginia.

And today was a joy beyond words. Mr. Billy Graham himself would be making a special appearance at the service tonight. I'd seen the very handsome Mr. Graham on TV many times. I loved it when he explained about God's plan of salvation, especially when he said that God would have sent His son to die for *me*, even if I had been the only person in the world. That He longed to be my personal Savior. That as His child, He had a special plan for my life. Mother and Daddy and we four kids were all planning to attend the crusade together. "Dear God," I prayed. "More than anything else in this world, I'd like to ask Jesus to come into my heart at that crusade tonight."

That night as we sang "Blessed Assurance," and all through Mr. Graham's spellbinding message, I reminded God that I wanted this Jesus he spoke about. When it came time for the invitation hymn, "Just As I Am," a soft wind washed over the crowd. I watched as a couple holding hands walked forward to accept Christ. A man stooped over on a cane soon followed. I followed, knowing somehow deep within me that my life would never be the same.

I arranged the red grosgrain ribbons on my long brown pigtails and began my journey to the stage. Down by the makeshift altar, I mingled with all sorts of people, all after the same thing I was: the promise of a personal savior and a home in heaven forever.

At the close of the service, a counselor assigned to each of us took us aside and explained the importance of completing the correspondence Bible study course offered by the Billy Graham Evangelistic Association in Minneapolis, Minnesota. "You will need to mail in your lesson each week, and then the instructor assigned to you will grade it and return it to you," my counselor told me. I'd sent letters to my aunt and uncle in Virginia but never had I licked a stamp on an envelope going to Minnesota. I couldn't wait to get started at my little oak rolltop desk. I loved to receive mail and I loved to send it. Pretty soon I'd be doing plenty of both. My outgoing mail would be clothespinned to our mailbox right along with Mother's utility payments.

The Bible study course stressed that we strive to memorize Scripture, to hide it in our hearts for a time when we would call on it to help us. One of the first verses I committed to memory was I Samuel 16:7: "For man looketh on the outward appearance, but the Lord looketh on the heart." That verse was to become my personal mantra, for at age thirteen, my face and left eye began to swell from mysterious tumors caused by something my doctors referred to as neurofibromatosis, at that time known as The Elephant Man's Disease. When one of the kids at school would make fun of my distorted face, I'd remember that verse and the arrow to my heart didn't hurt quite so badly. One day I had a seizure in gym class and a fellow student yelled "epileptic" to a snickering crowd of kids. I called on this Savior of mine as never before and remembered those Bible verses sequestered deep in my heart. "You're right there, looking on the *inside* of me, aren't You, God?" I asked. And I could feel Him answering with a great big yes and the biggest hug ever.

As tumors appeared all over my body, the effects of the hormonal changes of puberty, I spent more and more time in hospitals and at clinics. More than once, it was a nurse's soft-spoken kindness that kept me hanging on amidst the frightening world of heath care. I began to pray: "If I were a nurse, Lord, I could share Your love with patients who are afraid like me." But there was only one big problem. With high school teachers questioning that I even *had* a future, I hadn't taken a college preparatory course. Rather, I had gone for "a business track," squandering the afternoons of my senior year selling Avon cosmetics door to door.

At the advice of a counselor at the Marshall University School of Nursing, I spent my freshman year of college completing the prerequisites for Nursing school such as psychology, sociology, anatomy, chemistry, and English in the hopes of proving myself worthy to be admitted to the Nursing program. I mastered everything but chemistry, which proved impossible for my artistic mind. One morning after I had failed yet another quiz, a pretty black-haired girl sitting next to me asked, "Why don't you come over to my house and let me tutor you?" I couldn't believe it. It was just as I'd heard Billy Graham once say on a television crusade: "When God has a plan for your life, He will place the very people you need in your path." Soon Jeanne Kouns was tutoring me in exchange for my babysitting her two toddlers and sewing kitchen curtains, two things that came naturally for me.

I earned a B+ average for my freshman year of college,

but I still needed something to set me apart from the other students desiring entrance into the highly competitive Nursing program. "Lord, show me what to do," I prayed. Soon after, when I formally applied to the Nursing program, they requested an essay on why I wanted to be a nurse. In that essay I chronicled my journey with neurofibromatosis, and told of personal encounters with nurses who refused to let me give up along the way. "I want more than anything to have the chance to be one of those nurses," I wrote. When I was notified of my acceptance into the Marshall University Nursing Program, I was told that my essay was the cream that had elevated me to the top of the application pile. That rare compliment gave me the confidence that if I gave nursing everything within me, and asked God to guide me, I could actually become a registered nurse. In May 1974, I realized that goal.

Over the next several years, I required numerous surgeries to debulk disfiguring and visually destructive tumors. While I was recuperating from one such operation, my mother noticed my depressed mood. She smoothed the sheets on my hospital bed and sat down beside me, taking my hand in hers. "I know having this disease is rough," she said, "but your adversity can be your opportunity." Right then and there we prayed that God would use me to minister to others who have my illness. It was just as I'd learned in the Billy Graham Bible study course, that God would allow me to help others with the comfort He'd given me. I was determined to do just that and armed myself with the advanced education that would give me a platform to do so.

When the discovery of the neurofibromatosis gene was announced in New York City several years back, I was asked to address physicians and other health care providers on "Neurofibromatosis: A Patient's Perspective." I have also authored numerous articles in lay and professional publications on the topic. Whenever I have the opportunity to speak to a group, whether at the national level or locally, I welcome the chance to share how God has been there for me every step of the way.

Since those early years, I have had to face faith-challenging fears and losses from tumors that have recurred countless times, causing me to live in severe pain. In each of those times, I have called on the Savior I invited into my heart back when I was nine years old.

Today I sit at my baby grand piano and play the hymn

"Blessed Assurance," remembering it all. That hymn is still one of my very favorites, especially now that I intimately know the Savior who provides that sweet assurance every single moment. I silently say a prayer of gratitude for Mr. Graham who introduced me to that Savior, who made His love seem so irresistible that even as a child, I knew I couldn't live a day without Him. "This is my story, this is my song," I sing out loudly and with conviction. "I'm praising *my Savior* all the day long!"

When the Crowd Jeered

Donn Moomaw

I've played a lot of football on a lot of winning teams. Cheering sections, old grads gone wild, a masterly coach who keyed the players to fever pitch—all a part of the picture. But I never saw such enthusiasm as united the Billy Graham Evangelistic Team that swept London on a tide of religious revival during last March, April and May—and came to a fitting climax that night at Wembley.

Before we arrived in England, Harringay Arena had been rented nightly . . . on faith. We had no way of knowing if we could fill the twelve thousand seats for a single night. We did not even know what our arrival at Waterloo Station might bring. Those afraid of "Christ in politics" had been publicly hostile to our campaign.

Yet our whole team of twenty-eight Americans

moved toward England in a winning atmosphere of faith, grounded on confidence that, "If God be for us, who can be against us?"

At Waterloo thousands filled the station to greet us. The crowd sang hymns and, when Billy Graham lifted his Bible and called "God bless you," that blessing echoed and re-echoed in a thousand throats. Hundreds of Bibles were raised high.

Someone later said that our London office, with its huge map of pins marking churches, looked like "the inside of a military headquarters at zero hour." Here, each church represented a prayer center. The mission: a crusade for Christ, which, with no other weapon than love and prayer, might well win the victory of peace on earth.

On the opening night at Harringay Arena, despite a snowstorm, every one of the twelve thousand seats was occupied. After a week of capacity crowds, 1,631 persons had come forward publicly to accept Christ.

When the campaign concluded after twelve weeks, 1,750,000 people had been reached. Ernie Hill, *Chicago Daily News* writer in London, commented on how the Graham team had stirred England, although "the British dislike emotionalism."

But the Graham team was not emotional. It was enthusiastic and sincere. A Christian group can't lose if it has the sincere conviction that Christ has to become more than a figure of history.

Team spirit was vital. We knew that in London, the biggest metropolis in the world, there would be many who would not, could not, come to Harringay Arena. So others—like me, Red Harper, Grady Wilson, Louis Evans Jr., Charlton Booth, J. D. Grey, Dr. Paul Rees, Dr. Wade Freeman and more—formed an auxiliary; we spoke at universities, schools, factories, hospitals, on random street corners and down by the docks.

My own greatest challenge came when I spoke on a street corner near the London docks. Except for the man who handled the amplifier, I was alone before one hundred or more men, most of whom were antagonistic. One was an avowed communist who had, the week before, sent sixty thousand workers out on strike. There was no faint resemblance here to the bright, eager university students.

With some heckling, I began to tell these men how Christ became a reality in my life.

It wasn't easy here, thousands of miles from the UCLA

campus in California, before a hostile crowd, to explain how Donn Moomaw, once a football All-American, campus politician, steady caller at sorority row, suddenly found that all the glitter and glamour he had worked for was empty. How, just after the UCLA-California football game in 1951, a girl asked that young woman to go with her to a Campus Crusade for Christ meeting.

"She was a pretty girl and I went," I told this London dock crowd. "Much to my surprise, I found myself really interested in what was said about the power of prayer."

I was interrupted by a loud heckler, and the rumbling seemed to grow. *Maybe I'm wasting my time*, I thought with a slight feeling of panic.

Then I caught myself up short. What I needed was more steam, a better effort. In a few quick seconds I thought back to a lesson learned at the 1952 North-South game in the Orange Bowl. I hadn't practiced hard enough before this game, and a very enthusiastic gent on the other team named Jack Scarbath quickly ran around me for a ninety-five-yard touchdown. He ran through me and over me. Passes flew over my head like popcorn.

At halftime I took a good inventory of Donn Moomaw—and didn't like what I saw. When you've made a decision to turn your life over to the Lord, you can't let down in any phase without letting Him down.

There, on the London street corner, was a time not to let down, but to get fired up. Prayer is the best way I know to build enthusiasm. While I was still praying, a burly oldster helped me. "The boy's had an experience," he said with deep conviction. "Let him tell us about it."

And I did, talking easily and with a tremendous sense of uplift to a now quiet, more friendly crowd. I told about my first exploration of prayer, the first doubts that come to everyone, then the gradual discovery that Christ had all the answers to my restlessness. Finally, the excitement of giving all of yourself to Him.

I can't honestly say that my words cleared up the antagonism, but I am willing to leave the final score in His hands.

Some of the students we spoke to on different occasions asked penetrating questions: Did I personally have to give up a lot to spend all my time in God's service? It depends, I told them, on how you weigh material gains against spiritual progress, and which is the more real, the more satisfying. I personally have a sense of immeasurable gain.

To many, the self-discipline that God asks of His disciples may appear a large sacrifice. It shouldn't, however, to any man who has ever played on an athletic team. On a football squad you learn first that exerting your own will isn't an asset. Try it next time your coach benches you, or the quarterback calls for you to go off tackle when you want to pass.

You learn to "give up" a lot playing football. In the sports world they call it "training." In theology it's "renunciation." Either way, you do have to give up something to achieve something greater.

But there is such a sense of adventure in it all. And so much can happen through enthusiastic, sincere and dedicated teamwork.

At the Stratford Court Hotel where we stayed, no meetings were held. Yet two chauffeurs on loan to guide us through London streets, the assistant manager and other employees decided that Christ was the answer to their problems . . . and to the world's. It didn't happen through contact with any individual, but through their daily exposure to the spirit of the whole team effort.

Shortly after the closing meeting at Wembley Stadium, Charles Potter, forty-three-year-old former secretary of the Communist party in Reading, England, announced to the press that he had resigned from the party after hearing two of Billy Graham's sermons. Mr. Potter had been a communist since 1938. If a team of twenty-eight can fire up the largest city in the world through enthusiastic love of God, what would happen if every person who claims Christ's name enlisted whole-heartedly on His side?

PART 3

Living Close to God

PRAYER IS NOT USING GOD; *it is more often to get us in a position where God can use us. I watched the deckhands on the great liner United States as they docked that ship in New York Harbor. First, they threw out a rope to the men on the dock. Then, inside the boat the great motors went to work and pulled on the great cable. But of course the pier wasn't pulled out to the ship; the ship was moved snugly up to the pier. Prayer is the rope that pulls God and man together. But it doesn't pull God down to us; it pulls us up to Him.*

BILLY GRAHAM

Inside Our Home

Ruth Bell Graham

One of the peculiar things about living in a preacher's family is the way strangers expect to see halos shining from all our heads. I say strangers. Our friends know better. They've seen little Franklin bite his sisters; they've seen Gigi and Anne and Bunny shouting or perhaps scrapping out on the front lawn. Our friends are fully aware that, for all our striving to make God the center of our home, life in the Billy Graham household is not a matter of uninterrupted sweetness and light.

And it's not just the children. Our friends might very well have heard me moan to my husband Bill about how I can never muster enthusiasm for doing dishes three times a day for a family of six. I love being a wife, mother and homemaker. To me it is the nicest, most rewarding job in the world, second in importance to none, not even preaching.

But I don't like washing dishes.

To me there is no future in doing the dishes, nothing creative. And they are always there after each meal. I've even tried placing a little motto on the windowsill above my sink. It's a motto I've had ever since high school, and it says: *Praise and Pray and Peg Away.* I made my dissatisfaction with the dishes a definite prayer concern and still I couldn't seem to dig up much enthusiasm.

But, as so often happens, my prayers were answered in an unusual way. I took sick at Christmastime. It was Bill, then, who had to take over and do the dishes.

What did Bill give me for Christmas?

An electric dishwasher.

That's not the end of the story. When Dr. James Stewart of Edinburgh was in Montreat this summer, we were discussing housekeeping as a divinely appointed task, and he told of visiting a Scottish kitchen. Over the sink were these words:

"Divine service will be conducted here three times daily."

Bill and I do try to make our daily duties a divine

service. Take, for instance, the job of disciplining the children. We try whenever possible to deal with our children's waywardness in terms of the Bible. I remember one time when Gigi, our oldest, who is nine, had to be disciplined. I've forgotten what the trouble was now. But that day I took heed of the proverb: Spare the rod and spoil the child. Gigi was sweet as sugar for three days after that, and then she came to me and asked, "Mother, why'd God ever create the devil and make me bad?"

It was a good question, although actually it's not too hard to answer. We talked about temptation. We talked about how if there were no devil, there'd be no test of our love for God. And we talked about the best ways to fight back, with prayer and with long talks with Christ.

The question of our relation to Christ is, of course, a very serious one in our house. When I say serious, I don't mean long-faced. You aren't long-faced when you talk over a problem with a good friend. But from the time they were first able to talk, we have tried very hard to teach our children that Christ is their personal Friend as well as their Savior. And then, having prepared the soil, we let them grow in their own relationship to Him.

We try to start this relationship with the children's first

nightly prayers. One time Franklin, who is three, was disciplined for continuing to pick up the cat by its tail, and that night he said in his prayers, "Please help Mommy to be a good Mommy and not shut me in my room anymore."

These first prayers aren't ridiculous in the sight of a child, nor in the sight of the Lord. They are a fine beginning. In time, we try to show our children, by our own example, the different ways to live close to God throughout the day.

With four small children, the unexpected is always happening, like the time I heard little Bunny, who is four, break into a scream outside. I ran to see what the matter was and found her older sister smacking her first on one side of the face and then on the other.

"What on earth's going on?" I asked the older child.

"I'm just teaching her the Bible, Mommy, to turn the other cheek when she gets slapped."

It took quite some time to straighten that out.

Nothing is ever rigid around our house. For one thing, Bill's away so much of the time. Then, we always seem to be having visitors, both expected and unexpected. We even have a small zoo to keep track of. We don't count the temporary boarders like minnows and frogs and lame birds.

As permanent guests we have: a canary and a "budgie"; two patient and long-suffering cats, one of whom is so ugly we call her Moldy; and a dog, an enormous Great Pyrenees called Belshazzar. Because he eats so much he reminds us of Belshazzar's Feast in the Old Testament.

Anyhow, with the four children and the animals, with guests coming and going, with travel, Bill's work, and just the normal household emergencies, a regularly scheduled time for worship is a bit difficult. Of course, we try hard to have morning family devotions and evening prayers, and always we have grace before meals. But I've long wished for a regularly scheduled private devotion period that makes a person feel she is living in the presence of God.

For years now I've found two substitutes:

One is daylong Bible reading, which seems as natural to the kids as my preparing meals. The Bible stays open in the kitchen or around the house all day, and whenever there is a spare moment, I enjoy a few minutes with it. When Bill is away and there is a problem, I find a lot of help in Proverbs. Proverbs has more practical help in it than any ten child psychology books put together. The thirty-one chapters in Proverbs and the thirty-one days of the month fit hand in glove.

Then there is prayer. Since we can't always seem to find one set-aside time, both Bill and I have learned what Paul meant when he wrote, "Pray without ceasing." I heard of a lady once who had six children and a very small home. She had no place for privacy. Whenever life got too hectic, she just pulled her apron over her head and the children knew she was praying and quieted down.

I don't do that myself, although I think it's a fine idea. Instead, as I'm busy around the house, dusting, making beds, cooking, sewing—whatever has to be done—I think of Christ as standing beside me. I talk to Him as to a visible friend. This is part and parcel of our daily lives so that keeping close to God becomes as much a part of our children's training as keeping clean.

Sunday, we feel, should be a day set apart. It is a family day for us, but even more, it's a day when we try to learn to know God better. It can be the most interesting experience in a child's life. We don't allow our children to play with their other playmates on Sunday, preferring it to be a family day. But we do have storybooks and coloring books, puzzles and games, all about the Bible. And we have special treats, like candy and soda, which they're not allowed to have on the other days. And we go up to our mountain cabin for the afternoon and sometimes for the night.

All in all, we have a wonderful time with no one but the family around, and somehow on Sunday there is a minimum of bedeviling and a maximum of very enjoyable companionship.

It seems to Bill and me that the word *enjoyable* would somehow be missing if we tried to go too fast with the spiritual growth of our children, with their halo-growing, as it were. We believe spiritual growth can't be forced without raising a brood of little hypocrites. We prepare the soil and plant the seed, and water and weed and tend the plant faithfully. But it is "God that giveth the increase." We're willing to take our time and let growth come from the inside, through Christ, not merely from the outside, through our puny efforts.

Yet, even if the motto I have out in the kitchen doesn't apply too well to dishes, it does apply to children and the problem of growing halos. Maybe the best thing, after all, is to Praise and Pray and Peg Away. The halos will take care of themselves.

Stormy Hearts

Rilla Scott

O'n my first day at work in the features department of a big Sydney newspaper, I collided head on with Peter Scott in the corridor.

Peter was everything I admired in a man. He had an attractive English voice, intelligence, a quick wit. And I soon learned that he shared my interest in theater, literature, music.

After being agonizingly aware of each other for about ten days, we dined out together. It was a perfect evening. In fact, the whole future looked perfect. Soon, we were radiantly in love.

Then the flaws began to appear. I was hurt when he joined in on cynical office jokes but because of my deep love, I kept silent. I was bothered by the abrupt way he spoke to simple, well-meaning but perhaps slightly inefficient people. And I was embarrassed to tell him that it was attending church that kept me from seeing him on Sunday evenings.

Only several weeks before, I had gone to a meeting of the Billy Graham Crusade in Sydney, drawn into the auditorium by depression over my failure to find work as an actress, plus fear of the future. When I walked forward to give my life to Christ, I realized it was the first time I was doing something for myself about faith in God, rather than simply accepting certain beliefs as an inheritance from my parents.

After this spiritual rebirth, I was given the courage to seek a job in a new field—journalism. But Peter was so brittle, so sophisticated, so witty, I was sure he would laugh our romance out of existence if I showed my true religious feelings. And yet the ringing pronouncement of the Crusade, and of my beloved church, was to put Christ first.

Put Christ before my hopes of marriage, before my love of Peter? It was a real test of my faith.

I couldn't make the challenge to Peter directly, not right away, not the way I could to other people I met. However, I asked him to dinner at my flat, and deliberately left my Bible and some religious papers lying about.

At first, he didn't notice them, but after dinner he casually picked up some Bible notes and read them. "What's all this rubbish?" he asked lazily. "Don't tell me you're one of those 'churchy' people."

So began what turned into months of arguments, discussions, fights, tears, furious departures from each other and later phone calls of contrition. Then new fights.

He wanted and needed me, but couldn't accept my "religious cant" as he called it. I desperately wanted and needed him but couldn't accept his cynical approach to God.

Then came the dreadful day at the office when I saw him open some bills, smile and toss them into my waste basket.

I was horrified at his lack of responsibility and cried out, "But you can't do that!"

"Why not?" he asked. "The system's worked so far. If things get too bad, perhaps I can pass around a plate in your precious church." My whole world seemed to collapse.

"I suppose there's no question of your marrying me now," he said. "You'd have to buy cheap cosmetics and bargain basement dresses."

Then, there came that one wild, violent, unbelievable night. We had another argument. Furious, Peter seized a favorite lamp of mine and smashed it to bits. He stormed out of my flat and, as he crossed the street below, I grabbed a script he had left for me to read and flung it out the window.

If it hadn't been so tragic, the scene would have been ludicrous—my lamp in pieces, his typewritten papers fluttering down two stories to the rainy pavement.

Weak and shaken, I lay on my bed and succumbed to great racking sobs. Was this what God had led me to? Loss of Peter just because I had tried to keep true to Him?

Then there was a knock at the door, and hope returned for a moment. Peter was coming back.

I opened the door, but from the fierce, tense fury in his eyes I knew that Peter was far from penitent. He wanted a book and some papers.

Not a word was spoken. We often had threatened to break up before. Now all links seemed to be broken between us. I sat quite still, watching as he looked for his things.

At that moment, I almost hated God for destroying—so I imagined—any chance of happiness with Peter.

But then I thought, had I really opened my heart to God when I'd been with Peter? It suddenly became clear that always I had kept God out of my relationship with this man I loved. I realized that this had been the reason we had had no harmony between us.

Then I knew I had to do something I had never done before, not with anyone, and it was doubly hard in Peter's presence.

But with the extreme relaxation that sometimes comes from despair, I just knelt by the chair and prayed. I prayed fully and aloud, I think for the first time in my life, with heart and soul and mind utterly committed to God.

Words poured out, and I'll never know quite all I did say. I know I asked God to forgive us, to pour love into our hearts and to fulfill His plan. Finally, I stopped but kept my eyes closed, waiting I suppose, for words of sarcasm from Peter.

The silence became so pressing that I had to look up—and there was Peter, sitting on the couch with tears in his eyes.

Looking back, I am overwhelmed at the sudden change God worked in our hearts that night. But it did not happen until I had removed the obstacles of pride and fear that kept me from being the type of person God could use.

When we were married, it wasn't all hearts and flowers, with problems automatically solved. In fact, some things became harder. Just as we were overcoming the last of the considerable debt, a joint business venture of ours failed with the loss of borrowed money. Peter tried to get back into journalism, only to find it a time of recession.

Yet it was Peter now, and the fervor of his prayers, that brought us both through.

Slowly, bit by bit, we are finding power and guidance to overcome the debt and the flaws in each other's character. My fears and doubts about being a good wife and mother, after years as a career woman, are each day gently but firmly being removed. And Peter's tenderness, sympathy and understanding toward others is miraculous to see.

Recently, we became the happy parents of a sunny-natured, beautiful baby daughter. The christening was a memorable occasion—one of the highlights of my life. Peter and I stood side by side in church and dedicated to

God our firstborn child, vowing to guide her, by prayer, teaching and example toward the deep joy and fulfillment we have found in the Christian life.

Away from Home
Joe Brillhart

Rochester, Minnesota. Mayo Clinic. So far away from our small Texas Panhandle town of Perryton. But, that's where the cardiologist recommended my daughter Traci go for an evaluation of the hole in her heart wall.

It had been two years since the doctor discovered the hole. She'd been pregnant with her fourth child at the time. After the healthy delivery of Kinzey, her daughter, Traci continued going to the cardiologist who had grown increasingly concerned. Along with the hole in her heart, he also found a leaking valve. He assured her it could be fixed a few years down the road, but with each visit he upped the time when the repair would have to be done. At one point, he even mentioned a heart transplant. Although they could do the valve replacement in Amarillo, the doctor felt Traci should go somewhere bigger with more resources. Mayo Clinic could see her right away.

On her first trip to Minnesota Traci underwent a battery of tests that showed not one hole in her heart, but *thirty*. Plus an aneurysm and the faulty valve. She desperately needed surgery, but the holes had caused the heart to work harder, enlarging it and hardening the muscle. They explained to her that her heart would have to be stopped during surgery, and getting the hardened muscle to restart following the repairs could be extremely risky. The only alternative was to try medication first to soften the heart.

The Mayo doctors and Traci's cardiologist in Amarillo coordinated the monitoring of Traci's heart while on the medication. No improvement after the first thirty days. Following another forty-five days, a slight improvement, but not enough to operate. Sixty more days on the medication could have dangerous side effects, but the doctors wanted to continue, hoping the results would outweigh the risks.

So many things tumbled in my mind during that time. *Traci's so young. She has four small children and Todd, who's a good husband. She's not even thirty years old. Her whole life is ahead of her.*

I'd grown particularly close to Traci and the kids, and we talked a lot. Of course she knew that family and friends were praying. Everyone at church too. But one day she said to me, "I just want to take a trip with Todd and the kids so they will have something happy to remember me by."

I just about lost it. Traci thought she was going to die. My prayers for my daughter became even more urgent.

"Lord, heal Traci," I prayed from my pew at the back of the church the next Sunday evening. That's all I could think of.

While others around me sang and listened to the sermon, I felt the words "I will heal her" as clearly as if they'd been spoken. They weren't audible, but the presence and assurance were so strong that I knew it was God. I couldn't wait for church to be over so I could tell someone. Tears ran down my wife Gayla's face when I explained what happened.

Traci had an appointment at Mayo on September 15, 2001. When the twin towers went down on September 11, we had to reschedule and wait. Many of the Mayo doctors had gone to New York, and flights were cancelled. It seemed an eternity till the end of October, but nothing could be done.

Traci and Gayla had flights to Minnesota a few days ahead of when Todd and I would join them. Two full days of scans and X-rays showed completely different results from the previous ones. More tests had to be done. The good news was that the aneurysm had gone. *Gone?* Traci said she felt better, but I suspected she was just relieved to finally be getting the surgery done. *If* the doctors thought she was well enough.

Todd and I arrived on the weekend before the tests would resume on Monday. Traci couldn't wait to show us around the Mayo Clinic. What an amazing place! People from all over the world with every imaginable thing wrong with them. The halls were more like a freeway filled with people instead of cars. People coming and going, having tests, and undergoing treatments.

We approached the waiting area Traci in particular wanted us to see. Great arches anchored the entrances at either end. The first archway had a group of men near it, so we continued down the hall. One of the men in the group seemed familiar to me. After a few more steps it hit me. *That was Billy Graham!*

"Wait," I told Gayla and Traci. "I think one of those men was Billy Graham."

"I doubt it." Gayla said. "I just read he had a broken foot or something out in California."

"I don't know who it is," Traci chimed in. "But one of those men definitely has something wrong with his foot."

Good enough for me. I spun around and went up to one of the men. "Excuse me, is that Billy Graham?" I couldn't believe I had the guts to do this. I'd certainly never done anything like this before.

Indeed it was. I introduced myself.

Slow and rich, his speech exuded his warm, southern manner. "What brings you here?"

I felt completely at ease and told him about Traci. By now, Traci and Gayla had joined us. He shook their hands.

"It's an honor to meet you. I will pray for you," Dr. Graham said.

Our conversation lasted only a few minutes, but it seemed as if the world stopped for that instant while we visited. *An honor to meet you?* Trust me, the honor was all ours.

People streamed by, none of them aware that right here was Billy Graham! How could he be invisible to everyone but us? Or had God just opened our eyes so we would be aware of him standing there with his colleagues at a time when we needed something to lift our spirits?

As short as the encounter was, we felt blessed and encouraged that Traci would be prayed for not only by the many people back home in Texas, but also a great and gracious evangelist. And, of course, Gayla couldn't wait to call everyone back home to give them the update on Traci and say that she had shaken Billy Graham's hand!

With the absence of the aneurysm Traci had to undergo a whole new set of tests for two days. The findings would be analyzed by a team of doctors who would then determine if the surgery would go ahead as planned.

On Wednesday, Gayla, Todd and I prayed while Traci went in for her appointment. Barely fifteen minutes later she came out grinning from ear to ear. The holes in her heart had shrunk to the size of tiny pinpricks. No aneurysm. The valve—working perfectly. The heart—normal sized. No surgery would be needed. The doctors couldn't explain it and said we were free to go home to Texas!

We filled Traci's prescription for the blood pressure medication she would still need and ate a celebration lunch. Afterward, we sauntered down a different hall, and once again, I noticed Dr. Graham. He wore a baseball cap and rode in a wheelchair, being pushed in the same direction we were walking. *He's away from home too*, I thought. *Needing prayer just like Traci.* Of course I wouldn't dream of bothering him again so we walked past.

Just as I got a couple of steps ahead of him, I felt an arm reach out. "Stop." He looked at Traci and Gayla. "How are things going?"

My immediate reaction was disbelief that he remembered us, but he had such concern in his voice. Compassion. Caring. A man who had a lot going on with his own life, yet he took a moment to reach out to us.

We told him the good news about Traci and that we would be going home to Texas. We thanked him for praying and wished him well.

Meeting Billy Graham still seems like a dream. In that moment when our lives intersected his, we felt God's peace and affirmation that He would do what He said— heal Traci. She could go back to being a mom, a wife, and living a full life. We were humbled that a man of Dr. Graham's stature would show an interest in us and pray for us. Especially since he was away from his home too.

What it all boils down to, I guess, is that maybe we're never that far away from home when we're with others who pray and believe.

They Gave Me the Melody

George Beverly Shea

Last fall when an allergy forced me to take a month off from my work with the Billy Graham Crusades, it gave me the chance to visit my eighty-three-year-old mother back in Syracuse, New York.

One night in her apartment at about 3:00 AM. I woke up coughing. I tried to muffle the sound to keep from waking her, but in a minute or two I heard her in the next room fumbling for her slippers. Mothers don't change: the same instinct that had her on her feet at a whimper from one of her eight babies was getting her out of bed now.

A few minutes later there was a rap on my door and in she came with a cup of hot tea and a plate of her own oatmeal cookies. Except for the white hair framing her face in the light from the bedside table, it might have been fifty years before.

I pulled on a robe and sat on the edge of the bed sipping the tea; she sat in the chair. For a while we didn't talk much; sometimes silence speaks best of all. Finally I said, "Like old times, Mother."

"Yes," she agreed, "I've spent a few nights sitting up with you."

Both of us were remembering an earlier illness when I was between ten and twelve years old, a mysterious infection that kept me out of school nearly two years—and turned an already shy boy into a monument of self-consciousness.

Big for my age anyway, when I went back to school and was placed in a room with boys and girls two years younger than I was, I wanted to sink through the floor. I'd never been a talkative child but now the founts of speech seemed to dry up altogether. Mother used to say of me as a teenager that I spoke only to answer a direct question, and not then if a nod of my head would do it.

The few times when I had to speak in public were agony. I remember once when I was seventeen being put on the program of a Sunday afternoon youth rally. In terror of appearing foolish, I memorized not only the words I was to say but the gestures, the intonations, the facial expressions. And then, of course, I stood up and fumbled the very first sentence. There was a snicker and my mind went blank. Not one word of my carefully prepared speech was left and, after stammering helplessly for a few minutes, I fled to my seat.

The problem persisted even after I had left home and was making my own living. Once in Chicago I was trapped into giving a talk. Wistfully I thought of my father's warm, wise, seemingly effortless sermons back home. A Wesleyan Methodist preacher, Dad always had been as fluent as I was tongue-tied. And then inspiration came. What if Dad were to outline a talk for me! I wrote giving him the subject and begging him to suggest some good points and anecdotes. "Don't fail me," I wrote, "this is an emergency."

Dad's reply didn't fill a third of the space on a penny postcard, "Son, God helped Baalim's donkey to talk so I'm sure He can do something for you. Love, Dad."

But although Dad would never do for me what I could do for myself, it was he and Mother who, with faith and love and patience, helped me at last to move beyond the shyness that would have robbed my life of any chance for service.

As Mother and I talked that night, the past seemed very close. I looked down at the teacup in my hands, the well-remembered pattern so reminiscent of other talks. And I found myself recalling other objects that her and Dad's love had endowed with special meaning for me. There were three in particular: the first was a piano, the second an altar, the third a straight-back chair.

The piano was an old Bell model imported from England in 1900 shortly after Mother and Dad were married. I first remember it, a small mahogany upright, in the parsonage at Winchester, Ontario, where I was born. Later it had the place of honor in other parsonages from Ottawa to Houghton to Jersey City and finally here in Syracuse.

The Shea family had no need for an alarm clock; our day started with Mother singing at the piano. The song we woke up to was this chorus from an old Kirkpatrick song:

Singing I go along life's road,
Praising the Lord, praising the Lord.
Singing I go along life's road,
For Jesus has lifted my load.

There was something wonderfully reassuring to us children about Mother singing at the beginning of each day, her resonant soprano ringing through the house. Dad loved to sing, too, and family hymns were part of our daily devotionals.

In singing I found a release from the old problem of bashfulness. Perhaps in the music I was able to forget myself for a while. At any rate as I grew older I poured out in song thoughts and feelings I had no other way to express.

Mother liked to leave little inspirational messages around the house for her children. On mirrors, dressers, hockey sticks, dinner plates, she would plant her words of wisdom: Scripture verses, poems, quotations from spiritual leaders of the day. For my notes she chose the piano.

I remember a poem I discovered on the piano one Sunday morning just before church. It began:

I'd rather have Jesus than silver or gold,
I'd rather have Him than have riches untold. . . .

As I read and reread the lines, it seemed to me that music swelled round them; in a few moments I had composed the tune for them that has since been sung around the world.

The second picture that came to my mind that night

was of an unadorned wooden altar. It stood at the front of the old, square red-brick First Wesleyan Methodist Church in Ottawa, where, when I was eighteen years old, evangelist Fred Suffield came to town to hold a revival. Night after night I listened to his stirring addresses, yearning to do exactly what he urged and turn my life over to Christ. But there was a catch: first I had to walk to that altar in sight of the entire congregation.

I was well over six feet by this time, gangling and awkward, and from the last pew in the church where I always sat in the hope of going unnoticed, the altar looked a million miles away. Dad sat down front on the platform during the meetings, but in his sensitive way, I believe he guessed the struggle being waged in the rear of the church.

The final service came. Mr. Suffield again gave the invitation. The congregation launched into the singing of the invitation hymn, "Just as I am without one plea. . . ."

And suddenly Dad left the platform, slipped down the side aisle to the back of the church and into the pew beside me. He said, "I think tonight is the night."

"I do too," I answered, and with Dad at my side I made that long walk forward.

It was the act that set the stage for everything that followed, though there was still a struggle to find my precise area of service. In sequence, I studied music at Houghton College, worked with a New York insurance company, married Erma, sang a little on radio, moved to Chicago to take an announcing job and met a young evangelist named Billy Graham. . . .

The final vignette focused on a straight-back chair. It was the chair in which my father sat the night he delivered his last sermon at Willett Memorial Church in Syracuse.

At age seventy-three, cancer had ravaged his body and left him too weak to climb into the pulpit. In the congregation, to hear him conclude fifty-three years of preaching, were his eight children and Mother. Though Dad's body was weakened, his spirit was never stronger. His sermon was one of great reassurance. In a sense, his words were much the same as those we found in a note beside his bed after he had gone. "Life has been wonderful," he wrote, "the promises of God precious, the eternal hope glorious."

I placed the empty teacup on the nightstand. It was still dark outside but dawn was not far away.

"God has blessed us in many ways," Mother echoed

my own unspoken thought. Her hands were gathering up the dishes. "Can I give you something more?" she said.

She meant tea, but my thoughts were still on those other things. A piano, an altar, a straight-back chair — music, and God, and hope eternal.

"Thank you, Mother," I said. "You've given me everything I need."

Baseball Daze, Radio Days

Ernie Harwell

*K*ids today are said to be members of the "TV Generation." But I come from a lost generation of Americans who were the "Radio Generation." We grew up on voices rather than pictures. We gathered around small electronic speaker boxes that gave us news of the world, fuel for our imaginations. Radio shows were family events—Fibber Magee and Molly, Charlie McCarthy, The Shadow, Jack Benny.

It was in a radio broadcast, *War of the Worlds*, that Orson Welles's Mercury Theater panicked a nation into believing we were being invaded by Martians. (Could TV have been so convincing?) And it was on radio that President Roosevelt told us about the bombing of Pearl Harbor. Long before television, radio linked us together in one big electronic family. It still does, I think.

Radio has been my life. I've been announcing baseball games for forty-three years, the last twenty-nine with WJR and the Detroit Tigers, and before that with the Dodgers, Orioles and Giants. Radio, though, has given me much more than I've been able to give back. It has made my life, and more than once it has helped change it.

Officially my résumé says I've been announcing games since 1946. But it goes back much farther than that. I called my first games in my little hometown of Washington, Georgia, when I was only six years old.

You have to know that baseball was an essential part of life back in that little town. We were all crazy about the game. Ty Cobb, the "Georgia Peach" and the greatest player of his time, came from our neck of the woods. My dad, Gray Harwell, a furniture salesman, played some ball, and I had ambitions of becoming a ballplayer myself. Our local pharmacist, Doc Green, had had a brief career in a semipro league and had actually played against the immortal Cobb, securing for himself the status of a small town sports celebrity.

On hot, dusty, Georgia summer days Doc Green's drugstore was where we all gathered round the radio to catch a few innings of the then minor league Atlanta Crackers, as announcers Jimmy Davenport and Mike Thomas called the action. To my young ears those broadcasts were a symphony: the crack of the bat and the smack of a glove, the hypnotic buzz of an expectant crowd, the distant bellow of a leather-lunged fan out in the bleachers, the cry of a vendor hawking red hots and roasted peanuts.

But the Crackers didn't play every day, and sometimes, for lack of anything else to do, Doc and my dad and the boys would lift me up on a stool, slide an ice cold fountain glass of Coca-Cola in front of me, and let my imagination—and my voice—run wild. Hunching over the counter, I'd use my glass as a mike, fix my eye intently on an imaginary playing field somewhere behind the shelf of Bromo Seltzer and give my six-year-old's version of a radio play-by-play.

"Folks, the Crackers are down to their latht three outs. Looks like we'll need some inthtant runs!"

The men at Doc Green's would grin as wide as Main Street. And when I'd get carried away with my description of the Crackers' do-or-die late-inning comeback, lisping and twisting my words like soft taffy, it was enough to reduce them to tears of mirth. They weren't being malicious. We were all just having fun.

"And Thmith thmacks a tingle to fenter! Tie game!"

Poor little Ernie! He just couldn't get his tongue straightened out. And the more excited I became, the more tongue-tied I got.

"Crackers win! How 'bout that, thports fans? Wow!"

Folks figured I'd outgrow my speech impediment. So did I. Instead, I became more tongue-tied than ever, and the harder I tried, the worse it got. It looked as though I would never meet the elocution requirements that were then a part of the Georgia public school curriculum. We were in the middle of the Depression, and there was no way my family could afford private speech lessons.

Yet, one day over breakfast, Dad looked at Mom and announced flat out, "Ernie has to get some help," whereupon I was given over to our local elocution teacher, the prim Mrs. Lackland. I still don't know where Dad got the money.

"Ernest," declared Mrs. Lackland that first fateful session in her plush Victorian parlor, "today we shall begin the serious business of teaching you to speak properly, and we shall not end our business together until we have succeeded."

For the next year, I was drilled by the relentless

Mrs. Lackland until I could correctly pronounce every phonetic sound in the English language. I declaimed poems, stories, newspaper accounts, recipes, the Gettysburg Address, over and over till I got them right; I flooded the plains of Spain with rain. It was hard work. At times I didn't know if I would ever get it right. But whenever I faltered or cast a boyish look of hopelessness at my teacher, she'd just say, "Let us try again, Ernie. I know you can do it. We are not giving up."

In the back of my mind was the notion that if I ever did get my words straightened out, perhaps someday I could actually be on the radio. Sometimes I'd even practice my speech by calling a game to myself.

In the end, the indefatigable Mrs. Lackland untied my tongue. I not only passed my elocution exams, I took the class prize, a little pin that for years I carried with me everywhere and is still worn today by my wife Lula.

While I was able to straighten out my s's, I never did learn to hit a curveball. My dreams of big league glory faded. But my interest in sports and broadcasting didn't. At Emory University I got involved in the campus radio station and started writing sports for the Atlanta papers. Then in 1946 after I'd done a hitch in the Marines,

Crackers owner Earl Mann hired me as his play-by-play man. I thought I'd reached heaven.

Now the boys around Doc Green's could hear me call a real game. Of course Dad was awfully proud, and nothing could have made me feel better than making Dad happy. You see, Gray Harwell had had some hard luck. While I was still a boy, Dad was stricken with multiple sclerosis. By the time I got the Cracker job, Dad, still a fairly young man, was confined to a wheelchair.

Dad was my biggest fan. Even in the heat of an extra-inning game, I kept a picture in my mind of Gray Harwell sitting in his wheelchair, his ear cocked toward the wireless. He was the listener I always imagined when I called the action, the person for whom my word pictures had to be absolutely clear. Sometimes I could almost hear him grunting through gritted teeth, "C'mon, you Crackers. Get us another run."

Frequently I'd kid him over the air: "Well, folks, that Cracker double play was in honor of the fattest man on Clifton Road!" Dad wasn't fat, but after he got sick, his rock solid body softened a little. He got a big kick out of my kidding him about it over the air, kind of a public private joke. I like to think that I helped make Dad's illness a little easier for him to endure. I felt I was repaying him for all those speech lessons he had worked so hard to pay for. In a way, I was reaching out through the radio to give Dad a squeeze on the shoulder.

Maybe you can say it was those boyhood radio dreams in Doc Green's that got me speaking correctly. But there was another, greater moment when radio changed my life.

Spring training, 1961. I was with the Tigers in Lakeland, Florida. It was the first time I'd gone to spring training without my family, and I was feeling a bit lonely. But I had lots of work to do. Broadcasters, like players, use those weeks in the Florida sun to work out the kinks. I had to get my voice back in shape, and I had to learn the names and faces of a whole new class of rookies.

On Easter Sunday morning I had the radio on in my motel room. Suddenly a voice came on. It was Billy Graham, speaking to a crowd at Peace River Park in nearby Bartow, Florida. I'd been hearing announcements on the radio all week about this revival, but I hadn't paid much attention to them.

Now—I did. I don't know why, but for some strange reason, without even thinking about it really, I snatched my keys off the dresser and drove the twenty miles or so over to Bartow. On the way, I kept the radio tuned to Dr. Graham's broadcast from the park. I didn't know why I was going or what for; all I knew was, I had to get there.

That day, I gave myself to Christ. I'd been raised in the church. I'd gone to Sunday school, Bible classes, a Christian college. Christ had always been a part of my life. But on that sunny Easter morning in Florida, Christ became my center.

And it's made all the difference. In 1981, when I was inducted into the Baseball Hall of Fame in Cooperstown, New York (no sports honor has thrilled me more), I agonized for weeks before the ceremony over what I would say in my acceptance speech. Finally I wrote, 'I praise the Lord here today. All of my ability comes from Him. Without Him I am nothing.' After that, the words just came. That's kind of the way it's worked out in my life too. As long as Christ came first, the rest just worked itself out.

Gray Harwell used to say that "baseball is a talkin' game," passed along from generation to generation. Words are the glue of its traditions. That's what baseball on the radio is. It's tradition. It's "Take Me Out to the

Ball Game" during the seventh-inning stretch. It's the distant crackle of static from a summer thunderburst. It's hot evenings out on the front porch, with your feet up and a pitcher of lemonade. Baseball is an announcer suddenly stumbling upon a nickname like "Dizzy" or "Doc."

It's a tongue-tied kid from Georgia growing up to be an announcer and praising the Lord for showing him the way to Cooperstown.

PART 4

Attention on Christ Himself

Billy Graham's Dilemma

John Sherrill

*M*ontreat is the home of the Billy Graham family. When I visited them recently, I was met at the door first by the barks of great Belshazzar, then by Moldy the cat, and then by the shouts of two of the Graham children, Anne and Franklin. Mrs. Graham came out last, drying her hands from a session in the kitchen.

At one point in our visit, Mrs. Graham mentioned the age-old dilemma facing any well-known minister: where does a preacher's responsibility to the public end?

In the Grahams' case this has become a pointed personal problem. During the summer months, entire busloads of sightseers drive up the narrow mountain road to look at them in their home. Mr. and Mrs. Graham are always polite but still face the natural desire just to be alone for a while.

"We're sometimes criticized for having too much personal publicity," Mrs. Graham said. "What our critics don't realize is how much we agree with them. Billy has always tried to get people to concentrate their attention where it belongs: not on the servants of Christ, but on Christ Himself."

Good News at Noon

Gene Beckstein

The possibility never entered my mind that someday I would be a teacher. In fact, the possibility was
slim that someday I would amount to *anything* worthwhile.

Born in the tenements of Buffalo, New York, I grew
up with no hope of better days. Violence there was a way
of life. When I was eight, the thunder of gunshots woke
me. Looking out the window, I saw a man die in the
glare of a streetlight. Oddly, it didn't seem that unusual.

We knew little of law and order. Even in our apartment, brawls often erupted. Our dad was a part-time
prizefighter and a full-time alcoholic. Combined with
seven brothers, that made for a real physical family.
Following the tradition, at thirteen I beat up a guy and
spent eighteen months in a training school.

After serving my sentence, I rejoined my street

buddies in stealing hubcaps—and anything else we could find. Later, many of them either died in jail or from alcohol and drug abuse, products of an impoverished neighborhood that knew only hopelessness and despair.

Somehow I scraped by in high school. Then, after trying a few no-future jobs, I joined the Marine Corps. Four years of military service opened a new door for me. For the first time, I learned that there was a life beyond the ghetto. But that life required education. The G.I. Bill paid tuition for veterans and I accepted—my one-way ticket out of the slums by way of New York University.

I was a twenty-nine-year-old college freshman when a friend tricked me into going to Rochester to hear some guys sing. He didn't tell me the program would be in church—a place foreign to me. After the singing ended, a giant Purdue football player spoke. John Ducharte was six feet five, 255 pounds and talked about being intimate with Jesus Christ.

Having played a little minor league baseball, I wanted to meet this dude—another athlete. After the program I walked up and shook John's hand. "Do you really believe all that rubbish?" I blurted out.

"I certainly do." John said, then added, "Do you have a minute?"

I followed him into a little room where he pulled out a couple of vinyl chairs. We sat down and he opened up his Bible. "Of course you know John 3:16, don't you?"

I lied. I said yes. John Ducharte saw right through me and started reading that verse from the Gospel of John, "For God so loved the world, that He gave his only begotten Son, that whosoever believeth in him should not perish, but have everlasting life."

Then he read Romans 10:13, "For whosoever shall call upon the name of the Lord shall be saved."

About then the door burst open and John's little four-year-old daughter swooped in. He didn't scold her for interrupting. Instead, he put his big arm around her and gave her a kiss. I was embarrassed. I had been taught that real men didn't do stuff like that, especially in front of another man!

Before I could recover, John's wife rushed in. "I'm sorry, John," she began. But he just put his other arm around her and kissed *her*. I marveled at that scene, those two muscular arms around his loved ones. This man had something special, something I'd never seen before.

After the ladies left, John asked if we could pray, this time putting that huge arm around my shoulders. When this guy prayed, I glimpsed *God*! For the first time I saw that it was possible for ordinary people, even street people like me, to get to know God on a personal basis. I cried.

"What's the matter, friend?" asked that gentle giant.

"I feel terribly far away from God," I managed.

He replied, "Good."

"What's good about that?"

"Because," he explained, "that's what Jesus is all about. He's the bridge to God. He's the mediator. You want God to come into your life—Jesus is the bridge. Would you like that?"

"I know I want whatever it is that you've got," I told him. Right on the spot I prayed to accept Jesus Christ into my life. And that life has never been the same.

Back home in Buffalo, I found an old, inner-city church where the people accepted me. Barely a month later, another door opened when I returned to Rochester, this time as athletic director at a youth camp.

Leading the Christian training there all week were young, just-starting-out Billy Graham, Cliff Barrows and George Beverly Shea. What a privilege for a brand-new believer, getting to work with those three. We were all put to the test, though, as rain played havoc with our schedule. I grumbled because I couldn't lead the outside activities I had planned; the youth were boisterous with no way to work off excess energy. Yet the Graham team remained calm and patient. I learned much from their worship sessions. I learned even more from their actions.

Without even trying, Billy Graham himself taught me two lessons in humility I've never forgotten. One night he came over and sat next to me, whereupon I felt I needed to impress him. I spouted off some Lou Gehrig statistics.

Billy gently placed his big hand on the Bible lying between us on the bench. In an equally gentle voice he said, 'Wouldn't it be nice if we knew Bible statistics like that?"

The next lesson required no words. During a rare free time, he asked me, "Did you bring your tennis racket?" When I told him I hadn't, he said, "I have an extra one," and we headed for the courts. Walking by his side, trying to match his long strides, my six feet two inches in height shrank significantly. Once into play, he pounded me unmercifully. *Me! The sports pro!*

I breathed a sigh of relief when his daughter Anne, just a little thing at the time, came running out on the court. *Oh good. That will give me a minute to rest.* Not so. Billy just scooped her up in his left arm and kept hitting that tennis ball back across the net. Beat me soundly.

One tends to remember lessons like that—but mostly one remembers the spirit of love in which they were taught.

When camp ended, I could hardly wait to tell others the good news of Jesus. My opportunity came soon thereafter when I landed a part-time job at a Buffalo radio station. Each day I did ten minutes of news, often bad news. Then—with a quartet standing by ready to sing Gospel songs or some businessman to give a Christian testimony—I'd say, "But hang on, we've got some Good News at Noon!"

After college, I migrated southward and devoted the next thirty-seven years to being a public school teacher, administrator and counselor. I coached high school baseball, basketball and soccer. Often, while working with students—students in trouble with the law or the school— I called upon the patience Billy Graham had taught me years earlier. And I called upon the memories of my ghetto days—the anger, the frustration. Most of those young people needed to know God's love just as I had.

I retired in Gainesville, Georgia, and returned to the ghetto. This time, however, I went to help *others* find a way out. My wife Margie and I sold our home across town and moved into a little house next door to the Melrose Housing Project so that we could be accessible to the people.

When I decided to start a feeding program at Melrose, Margie made the meatloaf, a neighbor furnished green beans and cornbread, and we put out the word: "Anybody hungry is invited to lunch." So it was that "Good News at Noon" was reborn.

I began working with all age groups, facing their many needs: countless hungry and homeless, gang-related trouble, drug and alcohol addiction, AIDS, frightened children who endure family strife. I saw again that insidious problem that prevails among those born into poverty, a problem I knew only too well—hopelessness.

I particularly wanted to reach the children, to somehow build in them self-esteem. I know how that child feels who gets on the school bus with not so much as a pencil, only to have to compete all day with children who sport shiny new lunch boxes. Remembering how John Ducharte helped change my life by telling me of God's love, I wanted to do the same for the children and their families.

Gradually, surprisingly, volunteers began to appear. Today, fifteen years later, they number in the hundreds—professionals and lay people, civic clubs and churches.

We receive no federal money. Instead, business groups organize fund-raising golf tournaments; schoolchildren collect canned goods; groups coming to serve meals bring the food with them; physicians retire, and then contribute their time, skills, and even equipment. All desire to share the Good News: The Gospel of Jesus Christ.

Good News at Noon now feeds hundreds every day, provides a homeless shelter, medical clinic and dental clinic. Volunteers teach, mentor and counsel. Each person who receives physical or mental help receives spiritual help as well. We tell each one, "God loves you. God's love can give you hope—hope, and help, for a better life."

God is blessing. Many lives have been turned around—drug addicts rehabilitated, jobs regained, families restored, little children playing without fear.

These are proud people; they just need a little help,

that's all. I try to serve them in a nonjudgmental manner, because someone once saw some worth in me. Thank you, John Ducharte.

And thank you, Billy Graham, Cliff Barrows and George Beverly Shea. Thank you for sharing with me the Good News.

Besides the early Christian training Billy Graham gave me, he continues to set an example. For in spite of advancing age and serious health problems, he just keeps going. And, at eighty-four and recovering from a stroke, so do I. Like Dr. Graham, I continue to minister in the name of Jesus Christ, sharing the Good News of Jesus Christ with yet another generation.

The Truth about Pressure
Al Worthington

I remember the occasion years ago in high school when I was asked to give a report before the student body. My heart was pounding so hard I thought I was going to die. Somehow, before a blur of faces, I stumbled through my talk.

Later I discovered that this kind of stage fright is fairly common. According to psychologists, the basic reason for such extreme nervousness is self-centeredness—or a matter of too much ego.

I didn't understand any of this in high school, nor later when I became a professional baseball pitcher. There seemed no connection at all between a speech before a large group of people, which I dreaded, and throwing a baseball for the San Francisco Giants before a big crowd of sports fans, which I enjoyed.

The situation changed when I became a late-inning relief pitcher in 1957. A relief pitcher must be ready to replace the starting pitcher when he tires late in the game. Often he is called into the most pressure-packed moment. It is a long walk from the bullpen across the field. Up to fifty thousand fans are shouting at him. Millions more watch his every move on television. No wonder this kind of pressure can make a player's legs go numb and his brain freeze with indecision.

When I took this long walk, it got so that my heart began to pound furiously, just as it did during that high school talk. My stomach felt as if it were being jabbed with hot knives. As a result, I often failed to do the job. Soon my stomach hurt so much that there were times when I was physically unable to pitch. The result was that during the next few years I moved from the Giants to the Red Sox, to Minneapolis and then to the White Sox.

The year of my big inner change was 1958. I was with the Giants then and we were playing at home at the same time Billy Graham was holding his San Francisco Crusade. My wife Shirley suggested one night that we attend a meeting. Why not?

When Dr. Graham began to preach, however, an

annoying thing began to happen. My heart began to pound harder and harder. In a clear voice the evangelist was asking us to give our lives to the Lord Jesus Christ. Inside I was saying, "He's not talking about me. I'm already a Christian. Why, I've practically grown up in the church. I've even taught a Sunday school class."

Then why was I feeling so much pressure inside? And when Dr. Graham made his final challenge for us to go forward, why did I feel such a strong inner desire to do so?

Just as I was about to get on my feet, another voice said: "Don't do it, Al. Someone might recognize you as a ballplayer. You can't afford to be embarrassed in front of all those people."

So I stayed in my seat, feeling dissatisfied with myself. Later that night we went to another ballplayer's home—Bob Speake's—where six of us talked for hours. I was defensive and repeated to them how active I was in the church and—yes—there was that Sunday school class I had taught.

Finally, one of those present turned to me and said, "Al, salvation is not something you earn. It's a gift from God."

That statement stopped me cold. It became clear to

me that I was a Christian only in the sense that I had accepted a faith passed on to me by my parents. Never had I on my own made a commitment to God.

Several nights later we went back to the Crusade. This time I did accept the challenge. I told Christ I was turning my whole heart over to Him. I was trusting Him. I was making my break with the old ego-centered life. It was a decision made with my mind, not my emotions.

One morning several days later when our team was to begin a road trip, I awoke with the most amazing feeling of joy. And enthusiasm. It also seemed that all my troubles were in new focus—and I had power to deal with them.

"This is what it is like to be born again," I said to myself. As I was leaving the house for the airport, I picked up our Bible. Eagerly I read it on the plane. It seemed so much clearer to me now.

I thought my troubles were over, but how wrong I was. Perhaps I was too zealous; perhaps I just used poor judgment. Regardless, I soon got myself in hot water.

First, it was with some of my teammates; in my new exhilaration for Christ I tried to interest them in Him. They were mostly indifferent or suspicious. One player began to ride me pretty hard.

Then there was the "binoculars" incident. This got a lot of publicity in the papers, and I don't want to dwell on it. Yet it raised a question of honesty that I, as a new-born Christian, felt I had to face.

In major league baseball every team tries to figure out the other team's signals—we call it stealing signs. It's a part of the game, and coaches and ballplayers on one team watch the pitcher, catcher and coaches of the other team closely for this purpose.

Someone on my team came up with the idea of posting a man in the centerfield scoreboard with binoculars to steal the signs of the catcher. He relayed the information to our dugout by pushing a button.

To me, this went too far. I felt it was cheating and said so to the manager. He disagreed and pointed out there was no rule against it. Now I am no "nice Nelly" type. I'll argue strongly with the umpire if I think he's made a wrong decision and I'll brush a batter back with a close pitch if he crowds the plate. Yet this matter of the binoculars fought with my religious convictions.

What was I to do? After much thought and prayer, I took a step that even some of my Christian friends thought was wrong. I quit the team. I simply felt that

God didn't want me to be a part of what I considered dishonest. So I packed my bags and went home.

It's a wonder my baseball career didn't end right there. The word was getting around in baseball circles that I was some kind of religious nut. So this period was certainly my lowest point. Yet I had taken the step on faith. It was done. I found a part-time job and resumed my studies in a nearby college where I planned to get a degree in education and then a job as a teacher-coach. Shirley and I put the matter of my baseball career in God's hands.

Perhaps in my heart I was not yet ready to give up on the idea of becoming a good major league pitcher. I was in my early thirties, an age when pitchers are at their best. And there was another reason. The change in my spiritual life had made a change in my emotional and physical life.

I first noticed it when I was asked to give a speech before a high school group. I had such a desire to tell these young people about Jesus Christ that I forgot about myself and my pounding heart.

What it proved to me was that the more I centered on Him, the less problem I had with my ego and with pressure. It also told me that I would probably be able to go into those tense, late-inning situations as a relief pitcher and not tighten up and lose my effectiveness.

So when a contract was sent to me from a minor league team, I considered that was my answer and signed it. I pitched well in the minor leagues for two years. It took that long to convince any major league team that I could help them. The Minnesota Twins gave me my big opportunity in 1964.

I wish I could say that the problem of my ego was solved once and for all. The fact is, it has to be dealt with every day. There was one occasion not too long ago when it came back strong again, together with my stomach trouble. I had been pitching well and newspaper stories referred to "Worthington's coolness in tense situations." My mistake was not so much in reading these stories, but in believing that I was as good as they said I was.

We were playing in New York. My stomach felt like someone had used it for a punching bag. I took out my Bible and read this passage in James (5:14): "Is any sick among you? Let him call for the elders of the church; and let them pray over him anointing him with oil in the name of the Lord."

I needed prayer. Who to call? I knew some active Christians in New Jersey, but pride made me hesitate. Finally I called Karl Helwig, who is in the automobile business and an active Baptist layman.

He listened to my story, then said, "My wife and I will be there in an hour."

When they arrived we went upstairs to my room in the Roosevelt Hotel. We prayed together silently for a few minutes, then Karl stood behind me, hands on my head. I felt the Lord's power flowing through his hands as I recommitted my life to Him.

The test came a few days later in Boston. It was the last of the ninth inning; Minnesota was leading 3–2. Boston had two men on base and there were two outs. I was called in as a relief pitcher to protect our lead and get the final out.

I forgot my stomach, forgot the crowd, forgot television. "Lord, this is just another ball game," I prayed. "Anything and everything I do is for Your glory. That's all I care about."

The count on the batter reached 3 and 2. My catcher signaled for a curveball. I was amazed. A curve was my worst pitch. I shrugged, threw the curve. Surprised, the batter swung awkwardly. Missed. We had won another game, and went on to win the American League pennant, beating out the New York Yankees for the first time in six years.

A new baseball season is just underway. I hope we win the championship again. But maybe we won't. Baseball is a game of ups and downs. Furthermore, baseball is not that important.

What is really important never changes: Christ's love for us. Our need for Him.

PART 5

To Faithfully Proclaim and Sow the Seed

A Visit with Billy Graham
The Editors of Guideposts

W hen plans were being made here at *Guideposts* to offer Billy Graham's best-seller *How to Be Born Again* as a book selection to our subscribers, one of our editors said pensively, "All across America, many people will respond to the message in this book. But some will not. I wonder what Billy Graham would say about the mental roadblocks or emotional barriers that hold such people back?"

"Why don't we go and ask him?" another editor suggested.

And so not long after that we sat on the terrace of the Grahams' North Carolina home with red geraniums nodding in flowerpots above our heads and birds twittering impertinently and the misty ranges of the Blue Ridge mountains in the distance. Billy Graham's attractive

wife Ruth brought coffee, and their big German shep-
herd regarded us benevolently as we talked on that cool
sunlit morning:

GUIDEPOSTS: Dr. Graham, in your new book you
outline certain steps that must be taken if a person
wishes to be 'born again.' Do you think there are some
mental attitudes or other conditions that make it difficult or even impossible for a person to take those steps?

BILLY GRAHAM: Yes, I'm sure there are.

GUIDEPOSTS: Could you tell us about some of the
major ones, please?

BILLY GRAHAM: Well, one of the first that comes to
mind might be called intellectualism, the tendency to
approach Christianity only from the rational point of
view. I think there are sincere people who have intellectual problems with the whole idea of a God-man Who
lived two thousand years ago, died at the age of thirty-
three, rose from the dead, and is our only way to salvation.
To the purely rational mind the whole thing is—well, it's
much like what St. Paul wrote to the church at Corinth—
it all seems like foolishness. Paul even used a word that is

the one we derive our modern word *moron* from. He said that Christianity can seem moronic to some people, because when man sinned against God in the beginning, man's intellect was affected. A veil is drawn over the eyes of people who refuse to "become as little children," and only the Holy Spirit can lift it. That's where the work of the Holy Spirit in salvation comes in.

GUIDEPOSTS: Can you give us an illustration of how this block can be lifted?

BILLY GRAHAM: Yes, of course. I remember the case of a man named Fred Smith, one of the greatest biochemists in the world. He was an Englishman who was brought over to this country by the University of Minnesota to do cancer research. Fred Smith was an avowed agnostic. He couldn't accept Christianity intellectually or any other way.

Now, Fred Smith had an American neighbor who was a devout Christian. They met each other, liked each other, became good friends. One day an evangelistic crusade came to the big stadium in Minneapolis, and the neighbor asked Smith if he'd like to go. At first he refused. "I was reared in the Church of England," he said, "and I've studied Christianity. I've rejected it, and I don't even want to think about it."

But the neighbor was rather persistent, and finally Smith agreed to go with him just once. So they went, and Smith was very impatient and scornful. On the way home, he said he didn't like the music; it was corny. He said that he didn't like the preaching; it wasn't logical. "The whole evening was a waste of time," he said. "I didn't get a thing out of it."

But that night for some strange reason, before he went to bed, Fred Smith remembered a verse of Scripture that had been quoted: "If thou shalt confess with thy mouth the Lord Jesus Christ and believe in thy heart that God raised Him from the dead, thou shalt be saved." (Romans 10:9) That's a rather long Scripture to remember, but he remembered it word for word. All that night and all the next day in his classes that passage kept echoing through his mind. He came home and thought about it that night. He talked to his wife about it. On the third night, without ever going back to the crusade, he got down on his knees and said, "God, I know there must be a Supreme Being. If this is Your way of salvation, I accept it. I accept Jesus Christ."

Fred Smith began to study the Bible as if it were a textbook. He grew in spiritual stature very rapidly. He and his wife became tremendous Christians. What I'm showing you is that God can take a passage of Scripture and reach the intellectual mind. The Holy Spirit lifted the veil from Fred Smith's mind. The preaching at the crusade that night didn't have to be clever, or argumentative, or even logical. Something was supernaturally done by the Spirit of God on the mind and in the heart of Dr. Fred Smith.

GUIDEPOSTS: There are certainly many such success stories. But what do we say to men and women to whom these revelations don't occur?

BILLY GRAHAM: Well, I think that we witness to them, but also we have to realize that the true communicator of the Gospel is the Holy Spirit. When I stand before a group of people, a small group in a classroom or thousands in a big stadium, I have a terrible feeling of helplessness. I know that I don't have the ability really to win those people to Christ. But I also know that I've got another Person standing beside me Who will do the winning if I'm faithful in my witness.

When the Gospel is presented, some people will respond and some won't. It seems at times that you could almost have identical twins standing side by side, one accepting and one rejecting. It's like the sun that melts the butter and hardens the clay. This is a mystery that I don't understand; it's part of the sovereignty of God. But I do know that when we faithfully proclaim the Gospel, His word will not return void. It accomplishes what God wants it to.

GUIDEPOSTS: The seed is sown, and some falls on fertile ground.

BILLY GRAHAM: That's right. Our job is to faithfully proclaim, to pray, to sow the seed, and that seed may germinate in many ways. I remember the Surgeon General of Portugal telling me how one day he looked down and noticed a piece of paper stuck to his shoe. When he pulled it off, he saw it was part of a Gospel tract. Well, through that fragment of paper he accepted Christ and became a real evangelical leader in Portugal.

Now, somebody had printed that tract, somebody had handed it out, never dreaming that it would win the Surgeon General of Portugal to Christ. And so we never know, when the Word is spread, what it's going to accomplish.

GUIDEPOSTS: Are there certain blocks in people's lives or actions that must be removed before such events can transpire?

BILLY GRAHAM: Well, there's a block that I see in people all the time that is far greater than the intellectual block. It's the unwillingness of people to commit themselves to the high moral demands of Christ. This is the most common block of all: people who just cannot say to Christ, "You will be Lord of all in my life, and I will stop doing anything that I know You would not want me to do."

GUIDEPOSTS: Do you meet such people very often?

BILLY GRAHAM: Yes, all the time. Just the other day a well-known person came to me deeply troubled, ready to accept Christ, but unwilling to give up the woman he was living with who was not his wife. And he was a married man. He said to me, "I have tried. I have prayed. I have wept. But I just can't let her go."

I said to him, "Well, this is your great test. You

have to be willing to repent of that sin. And repentance means "turning away from." In a very small way, I can understand the struggle you're going through, because when I first came to Christ I was going with a girl who was not a Christian, and she was unwilling to become one. I was very much in love with her, or so I thought, but the Lord seemed to be telling me that this was my big test—was I willing to give up the girl, or was I not?

I remember the night I went over and told her that we had to stop seeing each other. We'd been going together for three years, and I'm sure we both had intended to be married. And I remember that when I drove home that night, about ten miles, I wept all the way. But I was doing it for Christ. Of course, I didn't realize then that the Lord had somebody else in mind who would turn out to be the ideal wife for me.

GUIDEPOSTS: Is this problem of sexual immorality very prevalent, then?

BILLY GRAHAM: I'd say that it is the one that comes to my attention most often as a force holding people back in their spiritual lives. They're not willing to surrender that area to Christ, especially in our promiscuous society where sex is exploited everywhere, on television, on newsstands, in books. If I were eighteen or twenty again, I'm sure that without God's direct intervention I would not be able to resist, because temptations are flung out in front of young people today in a way we didn't know in my generation.

GUIDEPOSTS: You're really saying that people flinch from making a total commitment, is that right?

BILLY GRAHAM: Yes, that's right. Someone has said that this is the age of uncommitment. There seems to be no great challenge in this country today. So many people are just apathetic, interested in their own pleasures, not committed to any cause. And the cause I'm talking about is Jesus Christ. Some people are not willing to say, "I'll burn all my bridges behind me and surrender totally— my will, my mind, my heart, my family, my business or whatever—all my goals to Jesus Christ." And that is what Christ asks of us: to burn our bridges behind us and say, "Christ, You and You alone are the One I'm going to depend on for my eternal salvation and for my daily personal relationships. You come before everything, and

I don't do anything without asking Your guidance and help."

GUIDEPOSTS: Perhaps one reason that some people don't do this is because they don't feel the need for such a commitment. They say, "I try to be a caring, compassionate person. I try to aid my community and pull my weight in society. I'm not unhappy the way I am and I don't feel any tremendous vacuum, so why should I make this revolutionary leap, this total commitment?" What is your answer to such people?

BILLY GRAHAM: In my experience, people who talk like that are usually middle-aged. Young people aren't so complacent; they have too many hang-ups to be smug about themselves. But complacency is indeed a block with older people, and a difficult one to overcome. Sometimes these people go to church and live fairly respectable lives and are quite pleased with themselves. What is lacking, very often, is a consciousness or conviction of sinfulness.

If my own salvation depended even five percent on Billy Graham, I would have serious doubts as to my salvation, because I know I am a sinner. I know there are sins of omission in my life every day. There are sins of commission. God demands perfection from us. He said, "Be ye holy, as I am holy." But I can't be holy. Not compared to God's holiness. Oh, perhaps I can be holy in contrast to some of my fellow men. But not in comparison with God. It's like a housewife who washes her clothes and hangs them up in the yard to dry. And then a snowfall comes, and when it does, the whitest sheet she has on her line looks gray and dingy in comparison to the snow. That's the way these complacent people really are in comparison to the holiness of God, which is absolute purity. I've had many people in this category finally accept Christ, but many more in this category reject Him.

GUIDEPOSTS: What can be done to shake the smugness out of such people?

BILLY GRAHAM: Sometimes it takes a tragedy or a near-tragedy in their lives to wake them up. A serious illness, perhaps, or a narrow escape, or the death of a loved one. Sometimes it's an awareness of the approach of the end of their own lives. Just the other day, a lawyer, a Christian herself, asked if she could bring her eighty-five-year-old father to see me. Now, he was in the exact category we're talking about—had been all his life. I said to him, "Mr. So-and-so, do you really know Jesus Christ as your Savior? Are you certain that if you died right now you'd go to Heaven?" He said that, just the week before, watching me on television, he had made a decision and had come forward in his heart. "Well," I said, "that's fine. But are you willing to bow your head right now and pray and make it definite?" He did, and the tears rolled down his cheeks. Why? Because he knew that he was getting near the end of the road and that time was running short.

GUIDEPOSTS: What are some of the other external factors that hold people back?

BILLY GRAHAM: I'd say that another very common block is plain, everyday procrastination. People put off making decisions. Accepting Christ is the biggest decision of all, but they put that off too. They say to themselves, "Well, I've got plenty of time. I'll think about it next month or next year. There's no hurry." But often there is a hurry. Life is a fragile thing. None of us knows when it may end for us.

My son-in-law was telling me just the other day about a couple he knew very well. The wife was a Christian; the husband was not. Oh, he showed signs of wanting to be, but he just kept putting it off. One night the wife awoke out of a sound sleep with the conviction that she ought to talk to her husband about this hesitancy of his. She woke him up and talked to him so lovingly and earnestly that finally they prayed together and he did indeed accept the Lord. Then he went back to sleep—and he never woke up. He just died in his sleep. It was as close as that. A matter of hours, or maybe minutes. I could tell you many such stories of people who hesitated until it was too late and others who made their decision literally in the nick of time.

So you see, there are all sorts of roadblocks: intellectualism, immorality, unwillingness to make a commitment, complacency, procrastination . . . those are the ones I've mentioned and there are probably others. If we had all the answers, everybody would be saved, but they're not saved.

Still, I know that when I've done the best I can and move on, the Holy Spirit stays behind, and I know He will carry on after I've left. That's what we have to put our trust in where salvation is concerned: the work of the Holy Spirit.

That's what it all comes down to, in the end.

Whatever Happened to Harold?

Harold B. Guiver

When my world began to close in around me several years ago, I told myself I was capable of handling the situation. After all, I had learned to rely upon myself since boyhood. I had gone into the investment counseling business on my own; I had competed successfully in tennis and had become an international bridge master, encountering some of the really agile minds of the country.

It began when we discovered that our fifteen-year-old daughter was on drugs. "I know how to solve this," I told my wife. I set up weekly psychiatric conferences for my daughter. I took strong measures in watching over her. I tried to show her love and concern.

Two years later she had left home, was a hopeless pill

head and was living with a needle freak (one who shoots heroin). The two of them were involved in a burglary ring, stealing enough to supply their habit. My cleverness and ingenuity had completely failed.

In the meantime my wife had become interested in the Christian faith. If this was the crutch she needed to carry her through her grief over our daughter, I reasoned, then I was all for it. When she later told me that she had accepted Jesus Christ as her Lord and Savior and turned her problems over to Him, I thought, *Fine, if it will keep your sanity.*

For me, I had to continue to compete in the "real world." Wasn't I my daughter's last hope? I continued to bail her out of jail, to be around to show her I cared, and to try to understand the boy she was living with. I certainly couldn't turn to religion.

Then, months later, came two startling developments. My daughter, now eighteen, was at her apartment alone one night, awaiting the release of her young man from jail on a drug charge. Through her mother's influence she had begun to read the Bible. This night she decided to watch the Billy Graham Crusade on television. Afterward she called her mother and said with much joy and emotion that she had asked Christ to come into her life.

The second development occurred at the jail. A Christian jailer selected my daughter's boyfriend out of thirty inmates and took him out of his cell into a private room. There the jailer told the boy how Jesus was the answer to his problems and gave him a Bible to read. When the young man was released and rejoined my daughter, he also became a Christian.

Meanwhile my business partner and closest friend had lost his eighteen-year-old daughter who died from an overdose of drugs. Shaken by this tragedy, he decided to take my daughter and her boyfriend under his wing. Against my advice he hired both of them.

Over the next six months, I remained aloof from the situation. Yet I could see that both young people were progressing rapidly and successfully in their respective jobs. They were entrusted with money and responsibility and became valued employees. In my conversations with my daughter, I perceived a humility and beauty that was beyond my comprehension.

Gradually I realized I was seeing a miracle! Instead of a phony, foulmouthed, self-seeking daughter, I was now faced with a transformed young lady, exuding sweetness, temperance, serenity and bubbling over with love.

All that was now left was something I had a terrible time admitting—that what my daughter had had all along was a phony, foulmouthed, self-seeking father.

Had I been living a lie? If what had happened to my daughter was real, then all my concepts of happiness and success, which included self-gratification, wiliness, exerting my will over others and obtaining material power were in error. I was really a miserable, lonely individual and didn't know what to do about it.

In the meantime the young converts had their union blessed by God in church and both continued to grow spiritually. I was beginning to explode inside. From every direction, I was now being exposed to real Christians who expressed God's love.

In March, 1971, I was competing in a bridge tournament in Atlanta. My partner was a woman who had not only a sharp mind but also a special kind of perception. When I decided to share with her the experience of my daughter, I found she was a strong Christian whose husband, Bill Lewis, was a regional director of the Fellowship of Christian Athletes.

Some months later Bill invited me to go to Baltimore with him and attend a Bible study group composed of professional football players and their wives. I heard some of them speak. For a person who always looked for reality, I knew this was real. These were strong men—pros—and yet they were gentle. Here they were, humbly confessing their inadequacies.

As I sat listening to them, I felt God's Presence there in the room. Inside me all the layers of ego, pride, arrogance dissolved. At last I saw clearly: What I thought was strength was weakness; what I thought was weakness was strength.

Later that night I asked Christ to come into my life and take over. And for the first time I experienced real joy. The inner loneliness was gone. His Spirit began to fill me.

For the first time since being a small boy, I now accept the fact that I am no longer my own boss. But it hasn't been easy to change deeply encrusted habit. I get down on myself too easily. I fall into old traps, then have to ask forgiveness before I can resume my journey forward. It's two steps forward, one back, then more slow steps ahead.

Yet I have that deep inner conviction now that I really am a child of God, that I am responsible to Him for the welfare of my loved ones—and yet I know we are all in His hands. And while I still do my best in every situation, it is great to know that my inadequacy is always His opportunity to show He loves me.

My Secret Heavenly Father

Connie Lounsbury

I was nine years old in 1950, swinging on our old tree swing, keeping an eye on my three little sisters playing in a sandy dirt pile nearby, when a stranger drove into our farmyard in a big black car. Mom came out of our rented farmhouse wiping her hands on her apron. Mr. Hanson introduced himself to my mother and invited us to attend his little country church that Sunday. He was dressed in a suit and tie and seemed nice enough, and my mother was gracious. But later when I asked her about attending church she said, "I don't have anything decent to wear."

The following week Mr. Hanson stopped in again and asked if he and his wife could drive our family to church the following Sunday. "No thank you," my mother replied with a smile, offering no reason.

"Then perhaps it would be okay if we stopped to pick up your two oldest children for Sunday school," he said. After looking at my eager face, my mother nodded an uncertain agreement. I had never been to Sunday school or church and I could hardly wait for Sunday. My ten-year-old brother Lee, however, was less excited.

I loved attending Sunday school, where I learned about Jesus. Later, Mr. Hanson asked my mother's permission to take Lee and me to Minneapolis with him and his wife to hear young evangelist Billy Graham speak. I almost jumped up and down with excitement. I had never been to Minneapolis and I liked being with Mr. and Mrs. Hanson and their daughter Sandra. They laughed a lot, hugged me sometimes, and held my hand as we walked into church.

The trip from our home near Orrock, Minnesota, to the big city of Minneapolis that day was long, but my excitement sustained me. We went into a huge building where the stage that Billy Graham spoke from was far from our seats near the back.

The music was wonderful, and I sang loudly along with more people than I had ever seen in one place. I am certain Billy Graham spoke long and eloquently, but I heard this simple message, "You have a Heavenly Father Who loves you very much." I couldn't believe I had two fathers. I wasn't sure my dad loved me. But Billy Graham said my Heavenly Father loved me. I wondered how that could be possible.

"Your Heavenly Father will always be there for you," Mr. Graham said. My dad worked in Minneapolis all week and only came home on weekends. Dad was never there when I wanted him or needed him.

"Your Heavenly Father will forgive your sins and make you pure again," Mr. Graham added. Sometimes I lied to my mother, and Mom said lying was a sin. I thought, *I should say I'm sorry, and then my Heavenly Father will make it okay.*

Mr. Graham continued. "If you are lonely, you can talk to your Heavenly Father. He will listen to you." My dad was so busy when he got home that he never had time to listen to me. He hardly ever even talked to me. My mother was too busy, or too worried about not having enough money, to pay any attention to me. We lived far out in the country and I didn't have playmates, so it always became my job to help care for my three little sisters. I felt lonely most of the time.

Mr. Graham kept talking. "Your Heavenly Father will love and protect you." I wanted to be loved more than anything. I wanted to feel protected. Billy Graham was asking us to come down to the front to say yes, to claim the Heavenly Father as our own. I wanted to claim that Heavenly Father.

The congregation was singing. *Into my heart. Into my heart. Come into my heart, Lord Jesus. Come in today. Come in to stay. Come into my heart, Lord Jesus.* Many people were leaving their seats and walking down the long aisles to the front where Billy Graham stood, while the rest of us sang that song over and over again.

My heart was so filled with the spirit of love and hope and the desire to have this wonderful Father for myself that I was overcome with tears and had to stop singing. Mr. Hanson leaned down to me. "Do you want to go to the front, Connie?" I was crying so hard I could only nod. He took my hand and led me down the aisle along with what seemed like hundreds of others.

When it became my turn, Billy Graham put his hand on my head and said something. I was so focused on his hand pressing gently on my head that I forgot to listen to what he was saying. But, I remember my whole body being filled with love. I physically felt different. When I walked back to my seat, I knew I now had a Heavenly Father who loved me; who would forgive my sins; who would always be with me, who would listen to my problems and who would protect me. I tucked that secret deep into my heart and carried that glow home with me.

Lee's answer to Mom's question about the rally was a quick, "It was okay." He grabbed his slingshot and was off to more interesting things, the whole event forgotten. My response was a little more involved, but I didn't tell Mom about my Heavenly Father. I had asked her once after I started going to Sunday school if she knew about Jesus.

"Of course I do," she said. "My grandfather was a preacher. He traveled all over the country preaching at several different churches, for all the good it did him. He lay in bed sick for months and then died as poor as a church mouse."

No, I didn't think Mom would understand my new wonderful feeling about my Heavenly Father.

The day that we still talk about happened several weeks later on a frigid morning shortly after Christmas. I was brushing my hair, huddled close to the wood stove that sat in the middle of the living room, trying to keep warm along with Lee and my three little sisters. Mom was in the kitchen cooking oatmeal. She called to Dad in the living room, "Bob, it sounds like marbles running across the floor upstairs. Go see what's going on."

Dad opened the door to the upstairs, where we all sleep, and started up the stairs. "My God, the house is on fire!" he yelled as he ran back down.

"Help me get the girls' coats on," Mom told Lee and me. "Take them to the Scheunemanns' and tell them to call the fire department and come help us. Run fast."

In my haste, I forgot to put on my winter boots and I soon found myself running in the subzero temperatures, through the snow, in open-toed shoes and anklets. Lee was carrying Judie, I was carrying Rennie, and Donna tried to keep up by hanging onto my coat. The Scheunemanns only lived around a curve and about a quarter of a mile down the road, but when we got there, no one was home. "They must be milking cows at Grandpa Scheunemann's," Lee said.

No one locked doors back then. We could have walked into the house, into the warmth and safety of their home. But it didn't even occur to us to do that. You don't go into someone's house unless they invite you in. You never go into someone's house if they are not home. So, we began walking the next half-mile or so to Grandpa Scheunemann's farm.

Later Mrs. Scheunemann said they had heard what they thought were calves bawling. When they looked, they saw "all five of the Duncan children coming down the road crying, the two oldest carrying the two youngest." Mrs. Scheunemann added, "Poor little Donna, barely six, so tired and cold she could hardly take another step. And there, a mile down the road behind them, a thick cloud of smoke telling their sad story."

The house and most of our belongings burned to the ground before help arrived. Family photographs, Mom's treadle sewing machine and a few other personal belongings were all they were able to pull from the house before it became engulfed in flames.

When Mr. and Mrs. Hanson came to pick us up for church on Sunday, Mr. Hanson said he had to blink his eyes several times to make sure he was seeing what he thought he was seeing. The house was gone. They learned that we were staying with relatives in another town, and came to express their sympathy. Later we moved too far away for them to pick us up for church.

Dad had been unemployed that winter and we had neither money nor household insurance with which to replace anything we lost in the fire. After a few days staying with relatives, Dad borrowed money to rent another old farmhouse and relatives gave us things they could spare.

We didn't have much before the fire, but I hadn't felt our poverty before. Now I stood in someone else's too-large dress, in that colorless, bare-windowed house with winter wind from cracks in the walls circling around my ankles. I set unmatched cereal bowls on a paint-spattered table and watched Mom stir oatmeal at the stove with tears sliding silently down her face. We had become paupers who didn't deserve better. My heart hurt so much I could only cry, "Heavenly Father, Heavenly Father, Heavenly Father."

Our family moved from place to place in Minneapolis —one rundown house or apartment after another determined by what new job my Dad got. He hauled rubbish, made roofing and delivered fuel oil, among other jobs, until he got angry at his boss and quit again. A part of me knew Dad was trying his best, but I eventually learned I could not count on him to always take care of me.

Through junior high, then high school, I depended on summer jobs and part-time jobs during school months to buy my own clothes and necessities. I sewed most of my own clothes. I also kept busy altering the hand-me-down clothing we always got from helpful relatives.

We never went to church. But when something especially good happened I knew where the blessings came from and I remembered to thank my Heavenly Father. He was the dependable Presence in my life, and with a simple faith, I tried to follow the Ten Commandments as well as my mother's latest admonishment: "Be a good girl."

I met David in early summer after my junior year of high school when I was working at a Dairy Queen. He had just returned home after serving three years in the Army. Shortly after we began dating I turned seventeen and he turned twenty-four. He was the most honest, sincere, wonderful person I had ever met and I fell totally in love with him. We became engaged in July and were married in October. Why would I need to finish high school? I was going to be a wife and mother.

David's dream was to own a farm and we decided to have children right away. Our first daughter was born thirteen months after we were married. In a couple more years we had three children, all under the age of three. I did a lot of praying during those years: for patience, for a good night's sleep, for the health of my babies.

By that time, we were attending church near the farm we had bought. I went to classes and was confirmed and baptized. I was finally making public what I had held in my heart for almost a decade—my faith in, and my commitment to, my Heavenly Father Who had been the central core of my life since that long-ago rally when Billy Graham led me to Christ.

And I realized that I wanted my children to have what the Hansons had given me: an education about Jesus. I wanted them to have what Billy Graham had given me: the knowledge that I was never alone; that I was loved and protected. As our children grew, I wanted other children in our community to know about Jesus too. As soon as I felt knowledgeable enough, I began teaching Sunday school and Vacation Bible School. I had come full circle from being a child in search of love and protection, and I told the children in my classes the same thing Billy Graham had told me fifty-five years ago: *"You have a Heavenly Father Who loves you very much. Your Heavenly Father will always be there for you.*

He will forgive your sins. He will listen to what you have to say to Him. If you are lonely, you can talk to your Heavenly Father. He will love and protect you. Just repeat after me, 'Come into my heart, Lord Jesus . . .'"

And now, after all these years, I look at my dear husband David, our four daughters, eight grandchildren and little great-grandson, and thank my Heavenly Father for showering me with such abundant blessings.

The Day My Faith
Meant Most to Me

Jeanie Kim Wickes

*D*id you ever stand on a street corner in a foreign country with your eyes shut? Suppose you didn't know the language of that country. How confused and lost you would feel!

This difficult experience was mine as a ten-year-old, blind Korean orphan on November 28, 1957. I had flown from Korea to Portland, Oregon, with ninety other homeless children. When I got off the plane, I was introduced to my new American parents, but I could neither see them nor speak to them.

The following six years brought me many questions and decisions but none as difficult as the one that faced me on September 21, 1963. I was a new student at Wheaton Academy, in Wheaton, Illinois, a private Christian high school, and after three discouraging weeks I didn't see how I could continue. I was living 160 miles from home and studying with the sighted, but without Braille textbooks.

At the end of three weeks, Mother came to school to visit me. After supper while sitting in my room, I told my mother something that I knew would disturb her. I wanted to leave school. "I've never gotten such low grades," I said. "I don't feel accepted here. Everyone is always so busy that I hate even to ask them to read my assignments to me. If this is the 'seeing' world, you can have it! I want to quit!"

Very, very firmly, Mother spoke these unforgettable words, "You've got to face the world. It'll never be easy. God has brought you this far in your life. Don't you think He will keep on helping?"

That night, while lying on my bed, I asked myself two questions: "Who am I? Why did I have to be the first blind person at this school?" To answer these questions, I found myself thinking back over the past sixteen years. . . .

I had lost my vision at the age of three during the Korean War. During and after that war, my father and I had been beggars. I remember endless days of walking the streets barefooted, begging for rice.

When I was five, my father, in desperation, placed me in a residence school for blind orphans. This school had been founded by Mr. and Mrs. Harry Hill, a Presbyterian missionary couple from America. They loved children.

At first I was inconsolable at the loss of my father, but it wasn't long until I grew to love the school. Singing became my constant hobby. We children sang in many city revivals where thousands gathered out-of-doors to hear the Christian message.

Life went on pleasantly until the age of ten, when a momentous decision faced me. Mrs. Hill told me that I had the opportunity to go to America. A home was ready for me there, and I had to make the decision. "Would you like to go?" she asked. "Although America would offer you better college and music education, would you be willing to leave all your friends and give up your Korean citizenship?"

This was a difficult decision because I loved my country and my friends. Also, I was afraid of the unknown. However, after much praying, I said a faltering, "Yes. I'll go."

Once I was established in America, many doors were opened. A teacher was sent to teach me English Braille. Nine months after coming to the States, I entered the public school in the fourth grade. Through the help of many teachers and my new mother, I sailed through courses from fourth-, fifth-, sixth- and seventh-grade work in two years. By the end of the second year, Mother, who had five other children, couldn't find the time to read all my nightly assignments to me. This problem was suddenly solved in 1960 when I entered the eighth grade of Indiana School for the Blind.

There, everyone had one common handicap, so nobody felt out of place. There were many advantages such as Braille texts and reference books, and understanding friends and teachers. However, one thing was wrong. By associating more and more with blind friends, I began to shut out the rest of the world. When I went home on weekends, I felt uneasy around my former friends. I asked, "If I associated only with blind people, how will I feel at a college where I'll be competing with the sighted?" After three years I decided to leave the school for the blind in search of a better preparation for college. I chose Wheaton Academy.

This school was like another world although it was only 160 miles from home. The difference between living at a school for the blind and at a private high school was shattering. In my old school I had been in the center of all activities, while at the Academy I felt a misfit. In spite of that, I kept reminding myself, "This is the best way for me to get along in the everyday world."

Still, things seemed to get worse and worse. Then came that evening with my mother and her firm words, "You've got to face the world. It never will be easy."

That night as I lay in bed I told myself that I wanted to obey her, but it seemed impossible. Yet I had put my faith in God during the Billy Graham Crusade in Indianapolis four years ago. From then on He had faithfully guided me. Now I realized that I was at a point of no return.

Desperately I uttered a prayer, "Father, if I can't turn back, give me strength to move forward. I try to make my own decisions, but fail. Take my life and guide me as You have in the past." At that moment a new confidence came over me.

Of course, since then I have had other problems to face and decisions to make. But everything has taken on a new dimension because I realize that God alone controls my life. September 21, 1963, is the day my faith meant most to me, because in recognizing my utter helplessness, I learned the importance of total dependence on God.

PART 6

God's Ear Is Open to Our Cry

Faith Strengthener

Billy Graham

rayer is the most important spiritual exercise that a Christian can have. If you are to live a happy, yielded and victorious life, daily prayer is absolutely essential. The apostle said that we are to "pray without ceasing."

Here are a few facts on prayer that may be of help.

First, the place of prayer. It is not the place, but the spirit of prayer that is the all-important factor. Jacob found that desert stones can become an altar. Peter prayed in a storm-tossed ship. Hagar cried to God in the heart of the desert. The Penitent Thief prayed from a cross. God's ear is open to our cry, whether on the seashore or on the housetop, on a mountain or a battle-field. However, daily prayer is better and easier under favorable surroundings. Ordinarily, it is best to have a place for daily prayer. Jesus suggested, ". . . enter into thy closet" (Matthew 6:6). It is good to pray at least once a day in a secluded place, praying out loud, guarding yourself against wandering thoughts.

Second, the posture of prayer. No particular posture is prescribed in the Bible. The Bible indicates many postures in prayer:

Lifting up of hands (Exodus 9:33, Psalm 28:2).

Sitting is another posture. David used this posture as mentioned in II Samuel 7:18.

Standing was the usual Jewish attitude of Christ's day.

Kneeling is a reverent attitude adopted by others. Daniel knelt three times a day. Stephen knelt and prayed. Peter and Paul knelt several times according to Scripture. I personally find this the best posture.

Third, the period for prayer.

Jesus seems to have devoted Himself especially to prayer at times when His life was full of work and excitement. The Bible says to pray at all seasons (Ephesians 6:18). John Wesley arose at four o'clock to pray. Martin Luther had to have three hours a day in prayer.

The Bible makes it clear that you can pray at any

time for God never sleeps, and His ear is ever open to your cry. The Bible teaches that there is public prayer, family prayer and private prayer. When Christ prayed in public, He was brief. When He was with the disciples, He prayed longer. When He prayed alone, He prayed all night.

God help us to pray! If we are to survive, we must have spiritual revival! If we are to have spiritual revival, we must have more earnest, effectual praying!

New Words for the Old, Old Story

Kenneth Taylor

❧

*T*he puzzled little faces surrounding our dinner table worried me. I had just finished reading from Paul's Letter to Timothy in our evening Bible session and had asked my eight staircase children to explain what Paul had said.

Silence.

"Well," I explained, "Paul tells us that as a soldier of Christ, we should do whatever He wants us to, and not just the things we like or want for ourselves. We should follow the Lord's rules just as an athlete must follow the rules."

"Why didn't you say that in the first place, Daddy?" asked eight-year-old Janet.

Yes, why? I wondered as I looked at the King James

Bible in my hand. The answer to the world's problems lay between its covers. Yet, so many people had difficulty understanding it. Not just children, but adults.

Next morning on the train heading for the Moody Press offices in downtown Chicago where I worked, I stared out the window pondering this problem. As a writer, I was especially aware of the importance of communicating thoughts quickly and clearly. And then the idea came—Why not write tonight's Bible reading in words the children will understand?

It was an attractive thought. The older children were twelve, eleven and ten. We were just graduating from reading Bible storybooks to the Bible itself. Taking out my Bible, I opened its pages to Timothy and began scribbling on an old notepad.

In the King James Version, II Timothy 2:13 reads: "If we believe not, yet He abideth faithful: He cannot deny Himself." *The children would have a difficult time with that one*, I thought.

I opened my mind to His inspiration, and then began paraphrasing the verse in simple, conversational style: "Even when we are too weak to have any faith left, He remains faithful to us and will help us, for He cannot disown us who are part of Himself, and He will always carry out His promises to us."

I struggled to say as exactly as possible what the Scripture writers meant, and to say it simply, expanding where necessary for a clear understanding. The Bible writers often used idioms and thought patterns that are hard for us to follow today. Sometimes their thought sequences leave us far behind. And often they compressed enormous thoughts into single words full of meaning, as with this passage from Timothy.

Even so, I found it enjoyable work. And when my train pulled in, I had finished the chapter.

That night I read it to the children. This time the older children could answer the questions.

The next morning on the train I tackled another chapter. Through the drumming of the coach wheels, a thought welled in my consciousness: Paraphrase all the Epistles.

Today I'm convinced the thought was put there by God.

Every morning, every evening I scribbled on the commuter train.

Even with a master's degree in theology and extensive

Bible background, I found it a challenge to transmit the exact meaning of the original so that not a jot of meaning would be changed or lost.

Summer, fall and winter passed, and finally I finished the Epistles. Then I settled back and read the copy. It was disappointing. It was rough in spots, and the great doctrinal thoughts were still not as clear as I had hoped for. It took a year to make the necessary corrections. Once more as I reread it, I was dissatisfied and penciled in many changes. This happened seven times and required seven years.

Finally I sent copies to Greek scholars for scrutiny. More changes.

At last in 1961, I felt the time had come to submit for publication what I called *Living Letters*. For, by now, I was sure they were part of God's plan. However, publishers didn't know this. One by one they turned them down.

One morning I shocked my wife Margaret at breakfast when I said, "Honey, I guess we'll have to publish them ourselves."

She looked at me quizzically. Our family had grown to ten children. And we had little money. Still, she agreed.

I found a printer, a Christian brother, who was enthusiastic about the idea. "Pay me when you can," he said. So I ordered two thousand.

Then, how to sell them? I took half a booth at the Christian Booksellers convention in 1962 and sold eight hundred copies. Encouraged, I sent out letters and samples to book agents.

Nothing happened.

This continued for four months. Now our family devotions included prayers for those remaining 1,200 copies. And then, four orders arrived in one week. They began to trickle in, in twos and threes. God seemed to be reassuring us.

Then God opened the floodgates. Someone sent a copy to Billy Graham. He happened to be in the hospital at the time and had time to read. He liked *Living Letters* and offered copies on his telecasts.

The demand was tremendous.

Accustomed now to the discipline of working on this in my spare time, I kept on. I tackled the so-called Minor Prophets. I knew they should be speaking to us today, but who was reading them?

Soon we published the second book, *Living Prophecies.* Then I left Moody Press, after eighteen years, to administer our own small publishing company. It was called Tyndale House after William Tyndale, the translator of the first New Testament printed in English.

Quickly we outgrew our dining room office and garage shipping room. We moved to rented quarters in the basement of a commercial building and two years later moved to our own modern building in Wheaton. Now I could give more time to writing. *Living Gospels* in 1966 was followed by *Living Psalms and Proverbs* in 1967.

With a dedicated staff we were able to have *The Living Bible* ready by the summer of 1971. Within seven months, 1.5 million copies were sold.

If someone asks me if the work was worth it, I only have to think about a twenty-three-year-old boy in prison who wrote me about how a preacher came into his cell and handed him *The Living Gospels*.

"In courtesy I took it," he wrote, "then threw it into the corner of my cell. Several times in the past I had tried to read the Bible but just couldn't understand it. However, one day I idly picked up *The Living Gospels* and became fascinated because I could understand what they were saying. It was through them I met the living Jesus Christ Who I have invited into my heart."

I thank God for the inspiration to begin and continue this work. I find myself constantly revising to make it even more understandable. So I will continue to spend my life in helping others find the universal solution for all troubled hearts—the Lord Jesus Christ. And I shall weep for those who cannot find Him.

A Brave Tear

Grady Wilson

I'll never forget the incident that occurred at Christmas 1951 in Korea. Billy Graham and I were visiting the wounded at a mobile army surgical hospital near Heartbreak Ridge, where heavy fighting was in progress.

We were ready to leave the tent when two medical corpsmen carried a young man inside on a bloodied stretcher. He had been wounded in the back and was lying facedown. Billy went to him, bent over and began talking while doctors prepared him for surgery. Unable to see the man's face, Billy lay down on his back and looked up into his eyes. "Would you like me to pray with you?" Billy asked.

"Yes, please," he replied. Billy prayed, asking God to strengthen and heal the man.

"Thank you and Merry Christmas, Mr. Graham," the young man said when Billy finished.

There was a momentary silence. All of us were tremendously moved.

Then a tear rolled down the soldier's face and fell onto Billy's cheek. Outside, Billy wiped his fingers across the wet place, and said, "That tear is the best Christmas gift I've ever had."

Out There Somewhere

Frank Richardson

For years Mother's Day was one of the most difficult times of the year for me. As a radio news announcer, each May I would find myself relating stories and reminding listeners that it was once again time to honor our mothers. I had little enthusiasm for it, because I could never honor my own mother.

The reason was that I had never known my mother. I didn't even know what had happened to her. My father refused to speak of her. When I was a youngster I'd ask him about her and wonder why she had left me, but his mouth would form a tight line and he'd look away. All I was ever able to get from Dad was that he had been married briefly before going into the Navy during World War II, and I ended up being raised by his parents in Richmond, Virginia.

Later, when I was seventeen, my grandmother, after much prodding on my part, got out some snapshots taken in 1942. They showed me, a toddler, with my young mother, who'd been only sixteen when I was born. But when I asked the inevitable questions, Grandmother merely sighed and said, "Oh, Frankie, I'm sure it was for the best."

The best? I wondered. Whose best?

Even after I had grown up, gone off to war in Vietnam, and eventually returned and began my work in broadcasting, the questions continued to haunt me: Why had my mother left me? Where was she now? Did she long for me as I longed for her? Or was I the son of a mother who did not want me and had never loved me? When I worked at a radio station in Richmond, for a time I tried to dig up some information about my mother. But I had no success.

In 1977 I came to my present job as morning news announcer at WTMJ–AM in Milwaukee. I married, and my wife and I had a son, Joey. I thought I could see my mother in his dark brown eyes. Mine are brown, too, and since most of the relatives I knew had blue eyes, I believed my mother's eyes had to be brown.

The years went by. After my grandparents died, my father was the only one left who knew anything about my mother. Despite my questions, he maintained his silence. Finally I gave up trying to break it.

Still, I would pray that I might meet my mother, feeling that she was out there somewhere. I would ask God to take care of her. And I would read my Bible, the one my grandmother had given to me when I was nine years old. Billy Graham and his team had signed it when I met them at age thirteen. The one verse that spoke to me was Romans 8:25: "But if we hope for that we see not, then do we with patience wait for it."

Was God telling me simply to wait?

In the late summer of 1985, for some reason the urge to find my mother intensified. One morning I reported for work as usual and aired a news item about the crash of a jetliner at the Dallas-Fort Worth International Airport. As I related the dramatic story of how a surviving stewardess, Vicki Chavis, had been found dangling from a seat in the rear of the L-1011, I couldn't get the thought of my mother out of my mind. I began to redouble my prayers about her. Finally, late on an icy Friday night the following January, my father called. "Son," he said, sounding a bit strained, "I know you've been wondering about your mother for some time. I, uh . . . well, I've always thought it was something that belonged in the past. But . . . here's a number in Fayetteville, North Carolina, where you can reach her," He gave me the number, then added in resignation, "I'll leave it up to you, Son."

I hung up the phone, dumbfounded. What had caused him to change his mind? I looked down at the number I had scribbled. It was much too late to call. I'd do it in the morning.

But would I? Should I? After crawling into bed, I couldn't sleep. Questions nagged me. Did my mother even want to hear from me? After all, as far as I knew, she had never made an attempt to get in touch with me during my forty-two years. Would my coming back into her life upset her?

And what kind of person would she be? Would I like her? Would I approve of her lifestyle? Would my longing for a loving mother bring the ultimate heartache: final rejection? Maybe I had better leave well enough alone. And yet . . .

I rose from the bed and got my Bible. It had helped me before. I settled in a chair in the family room and snapped on a lamp. Opening the cover, I noted a verse reference—Matthew 6:33—penned by Grady Wilson, an associate evangelist with Billy Graham. The verse was from Christ's Sermon on the Mount, and I began reading it. Even though I had read it many times before, I felt something in it would speak to my present need: "But seek ye first the kingdom of God, and His righteousness; and all these things shall be added unto you."

I felt assured that seeking my mother was right. Then I read on, and another verse really hit me: "Judge not, that ye be not judged."

Was I prejudging what had happened in the past? Was I letting a fearful imagination cancel out contacting my mother? How could I know her thoughts?

Early Saturday morning, January 18, 1986, I called. Two rings . . .

"Hello," came a soft Southern voice.

My voice was uncharacteristically shaky for a news announcer. "Is this Clara?"

"Yes, it is."

Suddenly I was tongue-tied. Finally I said, "I love you."

For a moment there was silence on the other end of the line. Then, "I love you too. . . . Who is this?"

"I . . . I think you know."

A long pause, and then she asked, "Is this Frankie?"

Three hours of nonstop talking filled in a lot of the gaps. I learned that my mother had been pregnant with me before she and my father got married. This had not set well with my straitlaced grandparents. Shortly after I was born my father left for the service. My mother, with nowhere else to go, stayed with my grandparents, who had little respect for her. Somehow they convinced the naïve girl, little more than a child herself, that they could do a better job of raising me. The marriage was dissolved and she went off to find a new life. By the time my father returned from the war, she had married someone else.

"Oh, Frankie," she cried, "I never stopped thinking of you. I wanted to find you all these years, but I wasn't sure what you had been told. I was afraid you had been told I was dead."

Mom went on to say that for some strange reason she felt a strong urge to find me about the same time my feeling about finding her intensified. The one thing that really inspired her search, she said, was the miraculous survival of her daughter-in-law in an airline crash.

"It was a sign from God," she said. "I felt that if He could save Vicki, He could help me find you." Her daughter-in-law was Vicki Chavis, the stewardess whose story I had related on my radio newscast. I had been reporting on a sister-in-law I didn't know I had!

Mom went on to say she had long pressured my father for my address through the years. "But he always felt it was better to leave things as they were," she said. When she heard I was with a radio station somewhere in Wisconsin, she had called every station in the state. She must have missed WTMJ or reached someone there who didn't know me.

"Then this January my church newsletter dealt with the theme Let Go, Let God," she continued. "I made those words my own, Frankie. I figured I'd stop trying to make our reunion happen, and just let it happen. And now—" she choked back a sob. "And now it has!"

That was more than six years ago. Today I not only have regained my mother—a brown-eyed mother who loves me and wants me—but I also have three sisters and a brother. And the uncanny thing is that when I finally met them, it was as though I had known them all my life.

Yes, it took a long time—forty-two years. But God did reward our patience. And today when I do my Mother's Day announcements over the air, it's hard to contain myself. You see, for me it's the happiest time of the year.

EPILOGUE

My Father's Message

Anne Graham Lotz

The week following my seventeenth birthday, my high school held the Baccalaureate, a Sunday service for members of the senior class, their families and friends. I knew it would be a memorable day for several reasons, one of them being that my father was guest speaker.

As I ran out the door of my parents' home, I told them I would meet them at the auditorium where the Baccalaureate was to be held. I then jumped into my mother's little VW and floored the accelerator as I dashed down the winding mountain road that led from the house. I knew I was running late, but I had promised to pick up some of my friends, to give them a ride to the service. As I rounded one hairpin curve, I came face-to-face with a great big, white Buick Riviera coming up the mountain.

It was too late to avoid a collision so I slammed on my brakes and jerked hard to the right. The VW went up a steep embankment, but not before that big Buick had crashed into the side of my mother's VW. I can still hear the crunch of the metal and the breaking of glass. As the rear wheels spun in the dirt, I tried to get out, but the door was smashed so I had to climb over the stick shift and exit from the passenger side. The lady who had driven the white Buick was standing beside her car, with an astonished, somewhat stunned expression on her face. I recognized her as our neighbor who was coming up to stay at our house while we were all at the Baccalaureate. I immediately apologized, and asked her help in pulling the fender off the wheel so I could continue my journey. Before I drove away I pleaded, "Remember, don't say anything to my parents."

Driving very slowly, I picked up my friends, and arrived late to the Baccalaureate. I parked the VW with the smashed side against some bushes in case somebody walked by, then asked my mother, "What happened to your car?" I ran to take my place in the line of seniors that was already marching into the auditorium. As I took my place on the sixth row from the front, with hair disheveled and mascara streaks on my face, I sought to look very generic in my cap and gown.

I don't remember much about the service except that my father marched across the platform, looked straight at me and then said to everybody in that packed Anderson Auditorium, "Anne has been a model daughter. She has never caused her mother or me any problems. It has been pure joy to be her father. We love her very much." I prayed I would die! As I bolted for the door when the service concluded, somebody grabbed me on the shoulder and said, "Anne, your father wants to see you . . ." Certain that judgment was about to fall, I went out to the front of the building where he was. He was surrounded by newsmen and cameras, all wanting to take a picture of my father and me on this wonderful and special day. (The next day the *Asheville Citizen Times* ran a front-page picture of my father adjusting my cap. The mascara streaks that ran down my face seemed to indicate that I was just emotionally overcome on this wonderful day!)

Finally, I slipped away, returned my friends to their homes, and went very slowly back up the mountain road to our house. I prayed as I drove, "Dear God, please have my daddy anywhere—he can be on the phone, he can be in his study, he can be taking a walk—just please don't have him where I will have to see him right now, because I just have to think this through. I promise I'm going to tell him—just not now."

I pulled up into the driveway, and carefully positioned the car so the bashed-in side was away from the house . . . and anyone inside the house who would happen to look out. I tiptoed up to the front door and opened the screen very carefully so it wouldn't squeak. I slipped inside the front hall, poised to run up the stairs to my room. I paused for a moment to let my eyes adjust from the brilliant sunshine to the darkened interior. When I focused and looked up, my father was standing right there! His piercing blue eyes were directed straight toward me. I hesitated for a moment that is still frozen in time in my mind. Then I ran straight to my father and threw my arms around his neck! As I clung to him, I sobbed, "Daddy, I'm so sorry. If you just knew what I'd done you never would have said all those nice things about me." I told him about my wreck—how I'd driven way too fast and smashed into Mrs. Pickering's car. I told him it wasn't her fault, it was all mine. As I clung to him and wept on his shoulder, he said four things to me that I will never forget . . .

First: "Anne, I knew all along about your wreck. Mrs. Pickering came right up the mountain and told me—I was just waiting for you to tell me."

Second: "I love you."

Third: "We can fix the car."

Fourth: "You are going to be a better driver because of this."

At that moment, I realized what an incredibly wonderful father I have. Because on that unforgettable day, my father taught me a life lesson about my relationship with my heavenly Father. The lesson is this: Sometime over the course of my life's experience, I would be involved in a "wreck" of some kind—a mistake or failure where I would get hurt or someone else would. Maybe something in my marriage or my career or my reputation or my relationship with a friend. The wreck might be my own fault or someone else's fault.

When that happens, the tendency will be to hide from God or to think that what I've done is so awful that He will turn His back on me. Instead, it's vitally important not to run away from my heavenly Father, or try to hide from Him, or to avoid Him, or to deny my responsibility, or to rationalize my behavior. *Run to Him!* I need to throw my arms of faith around Him, and confess my sin. Just pour out my heart and tell Him about the trouble I'm in and the mess I've made.

And if I listen very carefully, I will hear my Heavenly Father whispering to my heart, "I knew all along about your sin and your mistakes and your failures. I was watching you when you made that mess. I've just been waiting for you to come tell Me yourself. I love you. I can fix everything. I can take your smashed-up life and put it back together again so that it's better than it was before."

And on that day, I learned what an incredibly wonderful Heavenly Father I have too.

As I have reflected on my father's worldwide ministry, I have come to realize that what he did for me on that day so long ago, he has done for millions of others. He has always spoken the truth, but clothed it in such grace and love that he has made God attractive so that sinners in more than 186 nations around the world have run to the Heavenly Father in confession and repentance. And they have heard Him whisper words of loving forgiveness and restoration: *I've known everything about you for so long and have been waiting for you to come to Me. I love you. I can fix everything. I can take your messed-up life and make it better. You can start over. You can be born again. Now. With Me.*

The message my father practiced in our home on the afternoon of my graduation, and the message he has preached from pulpits all over the world, is the same. Lives have been changed, not because of my father, but because of his message. It's the message of God's love for sinners. It's the Gospel of Jesus Christ.